Weaving a Life of Faith with Social Justice

Weaving a Life of Faith with Social Justice: Church Women United in Seattle and Beyond

By

Phyllis Ilene Ratcliff-Beaumonte

Weaving a Life of Faith with Social Justice:
Church Women United in Seattle and Beyond

Published in the United States of America
Phyllis Ilene Ratcliff-Beaumonte
Seattle, Washington
Contact: phyllis_beaumonte@yahoo.com

(425) 255-5219

Cover design by Kurt Lorenz

All Rights Reserved

Library of Congress Catalogue Number: 2014919780

ISBN: 978-0-9640059-1-4

First Printing: December 2014

Printed in the United States by Morris Publishing®
3212 East Highway 30
Kearney, NE 68847
1-800-650-7888

DEDICATION

This book is dedicated to women who respond to the opportunity to transform lives and alleviate human suffering through the love of Christ and the Spirit of God. May each generation of women let their light shine in a troubled world, until He returns.

ACKNOWLEDGEMENTS

I thank God and the Holy Spirit for giving me the desire to write this book; Catherine Smith for her editing, insight, and encouragement; Dr. William Cate and his wife Dr. Jan Cate for their literary resource; Dr. Michael Kinnamon, former General Secretary of the National Council of Churches, for providing a deeper understanding of the historical role of Women in the World Council of Churches; my brother, the late Richard L. Ratcliff, Sr., and my niece, Mrs. Pamela Crallie Hines, for their love and encouragement.

FOREWORD

No better person can tell the story of Church Women United in Washington State than its former President, the Rev. Dr. Phyllis Beaumonte. Dr. Beaumonte's two passions combine in this book: furthering the ecumenical movement, churches working together in a spirit of fellowship and prayer for progressive social change; and confronting racism to end racial disparities—so needed today in the areas of education, housing, and jobs. Dr. Beaumonte's life has been an embodiment of these two interrelated movements. Church Woman United, now joined in its work with 26 denominations, has served since World War II, as the preeminent forum for racially, culturally, and theologically inclusive women who seek peace with justice in the world.

Dr. Beaumonte is an historian, educator, minister, advocate, and leader who knows how to share a story as important as that of Church Women United. She knows because she has lived it and because she is articulate, perceptive, and persistent.

I am personally indebted to Dr. Beaumonte for her tenure and guidance as a senior board member of the Church Council of Greater Seattle and for her generous and broad service at Mt. Zion Baptist Church.

Church Woman United and organizations with a similar pioneering vision have a pivotal role to play in the building up of our communities today. Enjoy this book—and be moved to action.

Michael Ramos

Executive Director

The Church Council of Greater Seattle

July 2014

Dr. Phyllis Beaumonte has written an extensive history of Church Women United from its beginning in 1941 in Atlantic City, New Jersey. Raising the question of why the Seattle, Washington, Church Women United closed with no explanation leads the reader to speculate on the history of the Ecumenical movement as a whole and on the future of women's organizations in general.

Including four theologians' perspectives on Liberation Theology and Social Justice gives depth to the book. Beaumonte's description of CWU as a "living movement" causes us to reflect on why one unit "died." The answers are complex, including an aging constituency and a lack of time for younger working women. However, the future is not as bleak as one might surmise.

Using Social Media, young woman and newly retired women are being attracted to embrace the mission and goals of Church Women United. The typical unit is changing to reflect the time constraints of women. Today, you will find units working on local projects involving women for short-term activities. The use of email Legislative alerts and Facebook pages helps the movement to stay alive.

This book is a well-researched treatise providing food for thought for anyone who believes in the power of what women can accomplish together.

Marilyn Lariviere

Church Woman United National President 2012–2016

July 2014

PREFACE

Seattle Church Women United (SCWU) was once the vanguard of ecumenical and social justice advocacy and an example of overcoming barriers to Christian unity. The city of Seattle was devastated when the unit closed its door. The citizens no longer had the opportunity to observe this witness of Christian women when they stood against unjust laws in the halls of city government, the state legislature, or when they demonstrated against injustice on the streets of Seattle. Many citizens in the greater Seattle area looked forward to attending SCWU celebrations such as the World Day of Prayer, World Community Day, and the May Friendship Luncheon. The void in faith-inspired advocacy for human rights and justice that the demise of SCWU has left still resonates throughout the city and beyond.

This book is written from my world view as an African American Baptist woman, who discovered early in life that Christianity is not simply a religion, church doctrine, or philosophy. It is instead, the application of the Social Gospel of Jesus Christ and the building of God's Kingdom on earth as it is in heaven.

One of five children, I was born to Albert H. Ratcliff and Bessie D. Buford Ratcliff in Seattle, Washington, at the end of the Great Depression. Those born during this time coped with the harsh realities of life such that this experience equipped them with self-determination and a belief that by and by things would get better.

Growing up in a Christian household provided me with a foundation built on faith in Jesus Christ, the Baptists' doctrine, tradition, and life's certainties. I was baptized at Mount Zion Baptist Church, Seattle, Washington, when I was twelve years old. Over the years, however, I wanted to understand God's larger cosmic purpose and what it is that God is bringing about in the world. The Bible uses such terms as the "Kingdom of God," the "Reign of God," and the "New Heaven" and "New Earth."

In 1989, I was licensed to preach, but it was not until March 1997, in Berkeley, California, that I was ordained by the Reverend Dr. Arnelle L. Jackson at the National Baptist Women Ministers' regional convention. Later I attended Seattle University's School of Theology and Ministry where I earned a Master of Arts in Pastoral Studies and a Certificate of Pastoral Leadership. I entered the Doctor of Ministry Degree Program at San Francisco Theological Seminary in 2009 and graduated with a Doctor of Ministry degree in 2012.

My passion to advocate for those suffering the oppression of poverty and racism increased, but it was not formalized until an opportunity presented itself over 35 years ago. Jeraldine Bright, an African Methodist Episcopal (AME) church woman, who was involved with SCWU, invited me to attend one of its annual Celebrations, the World Day of Prayer. There, I observed Christian women of all races, nationalities, ethnicities, socioeconomic classes, mainline Protestants, Greek Orthodox, and Catholic women united by their faith in God. Together they studied, worshiped, prayed, and advocated for justice. I was so moved by what I witnessed that I became a SCWU member, joining a community of witnesses to God's love, unity, and faith in Jesus Christ. Becoming involved with this ecumenical movement was my call to outreach ministry.

After joining the unit, my involvement evolved deliberately. I became chairperson of the SCWU Social Action Committee, was elected to the executive board, served as president of SCWU, and became president of Washington/Northern Idaho CWU. In addition I was a member of the national Nominating Committee, President of The Church Council of Greater

Seattle's Board of Directors, and the Chairperson of Religious Affairs for the Seattle Chapter of the National Association for the Advancement of Colored People (NAACP).

In 1983, I attended the global Sixth Assembly of the World Council of Churches. Held every eight years, the Assembly was located at the University of British Columbia in Vancouver, B. C. The Assembly's theme was "Jesus Christ—The Life of the World."

The experience was phenomenal. At the opening, I glanced inside the worship tent and saw a mixture of clothing and colors that represented the diversity among the 300 member churches of the world's largest religious organization. In complete wonder, I witnessed the manifestation of the Holy Spirit that transcended language, race, ethnicity, and economic and social status. I was very much in awe at the appearances of the Greek and Russian Orthodox delegates, the charismatic presence of Dr. Philip Potter, the General Secretary of the WCC, and Bishop Tutu, who made a compassionate plea for help in combating the evil system of Apartheid in South Africa. This historical ecumenical prayer and worship service included the Eucharist led by the Archbishop of Canterbury of the Church of England. We had a glorious time celebrating our oneness in Christ.

In addition to doctrinal and theological issues, the struggle to overcome biological and other human divisions was addressed. The social gospel's emphasis, by the African American Baptists delegates at the assembly, tended to play a positive role in taking on the challenge of inequality.

Racism and classism were determined to be hindrances to the unity of the local and global church. In answering the call to challenge individual and institutional racism, I had the privilege of caucusing with delegates such as Rev. C. T. Vivian, the recent recipient of the 2013 Presidential Medal of Freedom; Rev. Franklin Richardson, Rev. Dr. Samuel B. McKinney, and Dr.

Mary O. Ross, President of the Women's Auxiliary to the National Baptist Convention, USA, Inc. Our charge was to discuss and write an anti-racism resolution. After a lengthy debate, the resolution was presented to the delegate assembly, which voted to make it a permanent part of the records of the 1983 WCC Assembly.

Years later, while attending San Francisco Theological Seminary, it was my good fortune to take a course from visiting Professor Dr. Dwight N. Hopkins. He and Linda E. Thomas co-edited the anthology: *Walk Together Children*. Included in the anthology is an essay entitled "Called to Be the Salt of the Earth" by Iva E. Caruthers. She writes about three challenging realities: the Culture of Amnesia, the Crisis of Leadership, and the Compromise of Mission.[1]

Caruthers relates The Culture of Amnesia to the West African culture which has an image of the Sankofa bird, whose beak touches its tail. She wrote, "it is a reminder that in the circle of life, we must always look back to move forward. This backward view of time and space is circular not linear, where a people's faith in the past sustains them in the present." This is why the story of Church Women United must be told to each generation if it is to continue its legacy and capture the hearts of young church women.

The story of CWU includes courageous church women such as Margaret Shannon, and others before her, who laid the foundation for such an extraordinary, inclusive ecumenical movement. You will find in its history former first lady Mrs. Harry (Bess) Truman who was a faithful member, and former Secretary of State Hillary Clinton, a recipient of Church Women United's Valiant Woman Award. There were also women in search of a deeper meaning to life, and women who suffered the injustice of patriarchal church structures that prevented them from using their God-given gifts and talents for the glory of God.

They too, received inspiration and affirmation through CWU's movement. Guided by the Holy Spirit, Christian women from all stations of life embodied the compassion of Christ and became His ambassadors as they demonstrated the Kingdom of God on earth as it is in heaven.

CWU founded Women in Community Service (WICS) in 1965, along with other women's groups, to recruit and screen young women for the new Job Corps. In the 1970s, first Lady Rosalyn Carter presented a trophy to Ruth Hunter, President of the St. Louis, Missouri, unit for leading the largest Meals on Wheels Program in the country. Her leadership covered eighteen communities. During that same decade, CWU welcomed Mother Teresa to its national office in New York City. Then, in the 1980s, CWU had the courage to undertake "Re-assignment Race," a national initiative that required each CWU unit to look within its own ranks and rid itself of the sin of racism. CWU's remarkable historical achievements are extensive and are included in this book along with my research and findings on the closure of Seattle's CWU unit.

It is my prayer that after reading *Weaving a Life of Faith with Social Justice: Church Women United in Seattle and Beyond*, more Christian women will be inspired to use their spiritual gifts and talents to transform lives in the name of our Lord and Savior Jesus Christ.

Phyllis Ilene Ratcliff-Beaumonte

October 2014

TABLE OF CONTENTS

TABLE OF CONTENTS (continued)

LIST OF ABBREVIATIONS

CCGS	Church Council of Greater Seattle
CWU	Church Women United
NCCC	National Council of Churches in Christ
NCCC	National Council of Christian Churches
SCWU	Seattle Church Women United
TCW	The Church Woman
UCCW	United Council of Church Women
UCW	United Church Women
WCC	World Council of Churches
WCCC	World Council of Christian Churches
WDP	World Day of Prayer
WDPUSA	World Day of PrayerUSA
WICS	Woman in Community Service
YCWU	Young Church Women United

xx

INTRODUCTION

The organization Church Women United (CWU), founded in 1941, has always held a vision of Christian unity that implies ecumenical, prayerful, justice-centered action. An American-based ecumenical movement, CWU was built on the principle of unity across racial, cultural, and theological lines. Christian women of all races, classes, and denominations were a witness to faith in Jesus Christ. They offered their witness through worship, study, action, and celebration. Enabled by the Holy Spirit, CWU still expresses the message that prayer, faith, and action are inseparable and each has an immeasurable influence in the world.[2]

As a living movement, CWU exemplifies the charge that each generation of Christian women must hear the voice of God in the cries of those who suffer from hunger, poverty, and systemic forms of oppression; once God's voice is heard, the women prayerfully respond to others' needs.

While the response to God's call might begin in prayer, it has frequently and rapidly moved into action to bring about justice. In CWU, Christian women found an opportunity to respond, in their way, to God's call. From its inception, CWU was a channel of world-wide interest and courageous involvement.[3]

Three structural changes shaped CWU's history: From the beginning in 1941 until 1950 it was titled The United Council of Church Women; in 1950, and extending until 1966, the group existed as United Church Women/the General Department of United Church Women of the National Council of Churches of Christ. In 1966 the name changed to Church Women United.[4] Currently, 800 local CWU units are active in the United States and Puerto Rico. Local units, including the now-closed Seattle unit, organized around their own by-laws, with the only requirement being that the local unit's by-laws could not conflict with those of the national organization. Each unit developed its own organizational style and programming within the framework, mission, and common goals of CWU.[5]

In 2007, the Seattle unit of Church Women United (SCWU) closed leaving unanswered questions and a huge void in the greater Seattle faith community's outreach. It was as if a precious tapestry, well started, was stopped abruptly in the midst of weaving. Complete answers may never come regarding the unit's closure—which leaves important threads of social justice, peace, ecumenical advocacy, and compassion dangling free. The situation cannot be reversed until deeper understanding, re-commitment, wisdom, and refreshed or new and younger members discover how best to complete the work so well begun.

Safe spaces for dialogue need to be created, and under-standings about organizational effectiveness incorporated into a renewal effort. When these efforts are infused with Seattle's women's prayers, gifts, and faith commitment, a Seattle unit could re-establish itself and complete a tapestry that reflects the ecumenical vision of CWU.

With so many issues to face to enable justice advocacy, one must sort priorities and determine what is essential to complete the design, and make the tapestry reversible with front and back being perfect images of the inspiration that began the project. Many challenges face those answering a call to use their gifts. Can Seattle understand its history in such a way that it can pick up the loose threads and renew its faith-based care for the least of God's children? Is reinstatement of this dynamic organization possible in Seattle?

As with many organizations, the historical or archived records only glimpse at the remarkable work that was completed. CWU was far more than smiling groups of women coming together around a banquet table. Photos don't begin to show the vitality and effort that has been put into the justice work that

CWU has undertaken over the years—not just locally but worldwide. This book, hopefully, will open up to a new generation an effective blueprint for ecumenical justice work in Seattle and beyond—and a new flowering of spiritual gifts and energy to sustain dialogue and work for social justice across denominations and races.

While active, Seattle's CWU unit offered an exemplary witness to love and faith in action. The unit provided to Seattle not only social service and social justice advocacy, but also intercessory prayer in the name of Jesus Christ, for those in need and those undertaking service to the community. Seeing Seattle's needs, SCWU members undertook a number of successful efforts. Two successful programs are Dress for Success—a project to provide clothing and incidentals for economically poor women scheduled for employment interviews—and the founding of The Church of Mary Magdalene, a program to provide shelter, food, clothing, and spiritual support for homeless women and children. Both programs are still active. A testimony to the vision and prayer of the SCWU unit, The Church of Mary Magdalene continues serving women 23 years after its doors were first opened.

SCWU also sponsored Women in Black, a program that continues in Seattle. Women dressed in black occupy a busy street corner in silent protests for peace and justice. In their silent vigil, women *speak* against wars or to urge resolution of local and international conflicts and the stockpiling of nuclear weapons. Their witness has been so profound that another Women in Black group now gathers in Bellevue, Washington, as witnesses for social change. These witnesses are protesting in an upper middle class bedroom community of Seattle, which has become, in the last 40 years, one of the larger cities in Washington State.[6] Most recently, Reverend Kelle Brown, has stood with Women in Black to draw attention to the recent unjustifiable fatal shootings of young African American males by police officers throughout the U.S.

This book of eight chapters will discuss, in Chapter One, Church Women United's background.

Chapter Two is a brief discussion of Church Women United's structure and governance. Also, introduced is the Washington/Northern Idaho state unit.

Chapter Three explores the history and mission of CWU through various lenses: historical, sociological, cultural, and theological. The topics will include CWU's formation and its unifying factors, structure, and social justice praxis. The period covered in the discussion of the national CWU encompasses the last fifty years—in ten-year segments.

Chapter Four discusses Church Women United and ecumenism.

Chapter Five investigates in greater detail Seattle's CWU unit. Data gleaned from this effort from 1985 through 2000, mimics national CWU's historical framework but in five-year segments. Also discussed are prominent women to the Seattle unit and some history of the Church of Mary Magdalene, Mary's Place, and Women in Black.

Chapter Six is an in-depth exploration of two theological perspectives: Liberation Theology and the social gospel. Four theologians whose social principles reflect the values of CWU will be referenced: The Reverend Walter Rauschenbusch and his development and application of the social gospel; Archbishop Oscar Romero's response to the suffering poor in El Salvador; The Reverend Dr. Mossie Allman Wyker, former National CWU President and feminist author; and Reverend Dr. Martin Luther King, Jr., civil rights leader who responded non-violently to individual and institutional racism in America. The chapter concludes with a synthesis of common themes that have evolved from each theologian's praxis of Liberation Theology and the social gospel.

Chapter Seven revisits the historical lessons learned regarding the closure of the Seattle unit of Church Women United as perceived through various lenses.

Chapter Eight contains a summary of findings and the author's closing thoughts based on Seattle's CWU experience. Outside factors possibly affecting the organization's efforts are also discussed. The chapter closes with an offering of topics for discussion.

CHAPTER ONE

THE HISTORY OF CHURCH WOMEN UNITED

Bringing the work of Church Women United (CWU) into focus for a new generation is important, and it is equally critical that earlier generations of active faith-filled women be credited for their hard work in translating Gospel values into social realities. Through private and group prayer and action, CWU's social engagement has been two-pronged: via social justice efforts at the grassroots level and in the halls of political power. CWU women have changed history and not only that of the United States. Their influence has been felt in the World Council of Churches and at the United Nations. The fact that CWU accomplished this and pursued ecumenical dialogue in the process seems almost countercultural given the history of political party rivalry and denominational separatism so often prominent in the U.S. One must conclude that prayer infused CWU's efforts. Through prayer the women reached a vision and formed a plan to live out Christ's mandate to love one's neighbor and aim for unity, in spite of any differences.

Because the Spirit whom Jesus promised supports the work of God, the women's faithfulness has prospered them. Without fail, CWU has read the signs of the times and responded in kind; to use a term in common use today, the women approached their work holistically. They realized that there was a time to discern, a time to implement, a time to celebrate each other and their accomplishments, a time to build and rebuild community, and a time to move on to the next needs for social action. This chapter presents a macro view of CWU from its beginning; this includes the historical, theological, cultural, sociological influences, and social justice praxis that led to its national formation.

1

The essence of CWU's ecumenism and spirituality noted earlier are interwoven in its social justice advocacy, celebrations, resolutions, policy statements, programs, initiatives, and theological support statements.

Although CWU's jurisdiction has been American based, from its beginning the movement was worldwide in its interests and missions. The movement itself was unique in ecumenical history because it began with women who were already experienced in working together across denominations in their local communities and states.[7]

Some women's groups were at least fifty years old by the time the national organization was being proposed in 1941. "They had come into being on their own momentum and had a variety of forms and names such as missionary unions, federations of church women, and local councils of church women."[8] According to the Federal Council of Churches, in 1926 there existed a total of 1900 of these local groups. Thus, ecumenical work in cities and states began almost one hundred years ago.

For church women, missions and publications were highly important in bringing women together. "In 1900, The World Ecumenical Missionary Conference headed by John Mott, invited Christian leaders from around the world to attend a conference in New York."[9] Representatives attended from many denominational women's boards of missions. The American women were inspired to share their vision of a world Christian movement with other women. Next, the suggestion came to prepare and issue joint materials for mission study which up to this time had been done separately by each of the denominational women's boards of missions.[10] As a result, in 1901 the Central Committee on the United Study of Foreign Missions was set up, followed by the establishment of a similar Committee on Home Missions in 1908. Subsequently, the two mission committees

2

merged and created a Central Committee on the Study of Home and Foreign Missions.[11] The Central Committee published courses and biblical foundational studies related to mission work, so that both locally and nationally women could learn about the lives of women in other parts of the world. The success of these endeavors led to a Jubilee celebration.

Jubilee: 1860–1910

The year 1910 marked the fiftieth anniversary of women's cooperative ecumenical local and global missionary activity. During the anniversary celebration thousands of Christian women from every denomination were involved with speaking engagements across the country. They shared information and reflected on Sacred Scripture. During this anniversary celebration, a Jubilee gift of a million dollars was donated by a benefactor. To administer these funds, the women established the Federation of Women's Boards of Foreign Missions; it was comprised of local and state missionary unions throughout the United States.[12]

Publications

In 1914, the Federation of Women's Boards launched another cooperative effort that would continue for many years. This effort "...rose out of a concern that Christian women, many newly literate, in Asia, Africa, and Latin America needed literature written in their own language...."[13]

Accordingly, the Committee for Women and Children in Mission Lands was formed, and after formation it published periodicals and books in many languages. In addition, training programs were developed for writers and editors. The women also edited and promoted the use of literature for studying missions. This venture was valuable because, in 1938, the Missions Education Movement emerged and created a training program for the mission study leaders. The movement also established the first regional school at Winona Lake, Indiana, to promote friendship across denominational lines.[14]

In the meantime, Church Women of America had already developed Christian colleges for women. In 1921, the group raised over $2 million dollars for housing facilities and staff for Union Christian Colleges for women in Asia. The fund was augmented by additional funds from the Laura Spelman Rockefeller Trust Fund. This funding enabled the women to invest in women's colleges in India, Japan, and China. Moreover, the ongoing programs of the women's colleges and the Committee on Christian Literature became a continuing commitment that extended beyond 1928 and eventually resulted in CWU's World Day of Prayer.[15]

The Church Woman Magazine

In 1937, *The Church Woman* magazine became the official organ of the following parent bodies: The National Council of Church Women, The Council of Women for Home Missions, and The Committees on Women's Work of the Foreign Missions Conference. The magazine proved to be a unifying force and a powerful instrument in interpreting the issues that were put before the Constituting Convention in 1941.[16] Today the publication is no longer in existence. The national CWU office now publishes the *ChurchWoman News* a bimonthly National newsletter sent out in February, April, June, August, October, and December.

Unifying Celebrations

World Day of Prayer

The call for days of prayer began as far back as 1887. Although the women did not travel overseas, it did not stop them from being concerned for those who were suffering:

Mrs. Darwin James, President of the Women's Board of Home Missions of the Presbyterian Church was concerned about the immigrants from Europe and the Orient, who had come to America seeking a new life. Believing that those who prayed continuously would become advocates for the powerless, she issued a call to set aside a day of prayer for Home Missions in 1887. In 1890, Mrs. Henry Peabody and Mrs. Helen Montgomery of Rochester, New York, both American Baptist women, visited Asia and saw the need for the education of women and Christian literature. When they returned, they established a day of united prayer for Foreign Missions.[17]

World Day of Prayer offerings supported the American Baptist Women who also traveled to Asia and helped found the Committee on Christian Literature for Women and Children. Following the Asian visit, the first interdenominational mission study book was published. Out of that book evolved the National Council of Churches Ministries in Christian Education.[18]

Seeing a need for a national committee to unite women in prayer, the National Committee for the World Day of Prayer took action in 1919 and created a standard day of prayer. "The call was for all church women to come together on the first Friday of Lent, as the World Day of Prayer, to pray for the mission of the church in America and other countries."[19]

By 1941, some 7,000 local World Day of Prayer Committees had been formed. They used the National Committee's World Day of Prayer materials and received their guidance; however, the local groups were free to make decisions on how to implement each program.[20] It was cause for joy when World Day of Prayer committees were formed in Canada, Great Britain, Australia, New Zealand, and South Africa.

5

The United Council of Church Women, formed in 1941, assumed the responsibility for The World Day of Prayer in the United States.

> The World Day of Prayer movement is maintained, and its mission carried out by Christian women of the designated eight worldwide regions: Africa, Asia, Caribbean, Europe, Latin America, Middle East, North America, and the Pacific to bring together women of various races, cultures and traditions in closer understanding and action throughout the year. The International Committee provides coordination of National and Regional World Day of Prayer Committees and plans that promote the movement and celebrations.[21]

Today, the World Day of Prayer (WDP) is no longer solely under the umbrella of CWU. CWU is now in partnership with World Day of Prayer United States of America (WDPUSA).

May Fellowship Day

Another unifying event, the May Fellowship Luncheon, began during the Great Depression when people were gripped by fears of becoming even more destitute. During its annual meeting, the Administrative Committee of the Women's Council for Home Missions agreed that something festive would inspire the women with hope that in the future things would improve.[22]

Thus, on May 1, 1933, a luncheon was held—and for four successive years it grew in attendance. By 1937, when the New York luncheon committee invited all Protestant women in the city to attend, well over 600 responded.

In 1938, church women responded to a nationwide invitation for all Protestant women to gather in their local communities to reflect on unity in Christian service. In 1939, the Home Missions Council proposed that the appeals be combined and invitations be issued only in the name of the United Council of Church Women. This decision brought them further along the path to uniting Christian women into a national ecumenical movement.

The leaders also established a threefold purpose for the annual May Fellowship Day luncheon: to strengthen (1) a growing sense of unity, (2) the joy of Christian fellowship, and (3) the power of Christianity in the day of need. Christian women in more than a thousand U.S. communities met. The United Council of Church Women continued this tradition, and in 1945 the celebration was officially named May Fellowship Day.[23]

In 1976, the program for the May Fellowship Day celebration included the Valiant Woman Award presentation. According to the CWU members' Memory Book "Each year, the award is given to a deserving woman who has helped build and shape her unit." When a woman is nominated by her state or local unit, the unit makes a contribution to the National CWU Fund for the Future in the name of the Valiant Woman Award nominee.[24] Among the more well-known award recipients is the Honorable Hillary Rodham Clinton.

May Fellowship Day is now called May Friendship Day; its focus is currently described as "Celebrating the intergenerational bonds among women." Not only do women gather to pray ecumenically, they also highlight contributions and gifts of outstanding Christian women in the community. Included in the day is also a celebration of the Fellowship of the Least Coin, a worldwide movement based on the power of prayer and the willingness to set aside a "least coin" for a country.

World Community Day

Another celebration, World Community Day, traditionally held the first Friday in November, focused on responsible corporate action for justice and peace. In 1943, during a meeting for denominational presidents and executive secretaries, Mrs. Albert Palmer, President of the Chicago Council of Church Women, made a motion that a day be set aside in the fall for the study of peace. Previously, the women printed their own studies but agreed that their unity would be strengthened by having one day of united study. Thus, Armistice Day, November 11, 1943, was set aside as a special Peace Day called World Community Day.[25] CWU's celebration days continue to be sponsored by local units throughout the United States. For local units these celebration days are an anticipated time of joy and fellowship.

Human Rights Celebration

Christians affirm that all persons have inherent worth and dignity. Thus, the Human Rights Celebration gives local groups the opportunity to honor those in the community who have been active in the field of Human Rights.

Other Unifying Efforts

The Christian Causeway

Building relationships with women of other countries is the primary focus of the Christian Causeway Program. For CWU, Christ is the Causeway; it is for His cause and by His way that the women go where God leads them. These women walk fearlessly down new paths along with their sisters and learn from new experiences.

Through the international causeways, Christian women have discovered what it means to survive in a world with limited resources. In lands of scarcity, they have witnessed the beauty of

8

God manifested in the lives of those who sought ways to share their spiritual gifts and talents with those in need. The type of help provided depends on the specific needs of the country visited. Living the day-to-day life with women in their countries, coupled with prayer and conversation, builds strong ties and makes CWU women aware of the critical needs of the missions.

The Christian Causeway Program has included the following countries or groups in the designated years: "Africa, 1966; U.S.A., 1967; Latin America, 1968; Spanish-Americans, 1969, Asia, 1974; Caribbean/USA, 1975; Eastern Europe, 1980s; Russia, 1984; Kenya, 1985, and China, 1990."[26]

The International Fellowship of the Least Coin (1956)

The Fellowship of the Least Coin (FLC), previously mentioned, is a worldwide ecumenical movement focusing on prayer and giving. Shanti Solomon, a leader in the Church of North India, brought into being the idea of an offering of prayers and money that would help women worldwide. "When women gather in their local prayer services or denominational meetings, they offer the least coin of their country to the fellowship group as a visible token of their prayers for reconciliation, peace, and justice."[27] The least coin concept made all women's contributions equal, rich and poor alike. CWU manages the FLC offerings, which are used to establish programs to promote peace.

The Committee on Cooperation

Created in 1937, the Committee on Cooperation drew together various interests and formulated a constitution for *one* movement to address concerns about value shifts and conflicts within the U.S. For example, although the Fifteenth Amendment was ratified in 1870, Jim Crow Laws in the South denied Negroes their voting rights through a system of rigged literacy tests, poll taxes, and other racist devices. A culture of fear and

9

sorrow permeated not only the South but other regions of the country as well. In this climate of fear, the Ku Klux Klan evolved and gained momentum. Its agenda was to acquire political power, terrorize, lynch Negroes, and turn the country's focus back to states' rights in order to continue the "separate but equal" doctrine.[28]

Major global concerns also surfaced. For example, in Germany, Adolph Hitler reorganized the Nazi Party and laid the foundation to build a German empire. Seeing this outbreak of bigotry and cruelty, Christian women, with a sense of urgency, began to organize into a national ecumenical movement.

After three years of negotiations, the Committee on Cooperation issued a call for a Constituting Convention in 1941. Hence, the United Council of Church Women held a Convention in Atlantic City, New Jersey, and proposed a national movement.[29] "Representatives of three national inter-denominational committees attended and considered the proposal: The National Council of Federated Church Women, The Council of Women for Home Missions, and The Committee on Women's Work of the Foreign Missions Conference."[30]

During the week that Pearl Harbor was attacked, the women who had met in Atlantic City, New Jersey, founded the United Council of Church Women (UCCW) following a unanimous vote that a new organization be formed. The United Council of Church Women worked tirelessly to integrate the work of the three interdenominational women's groups from seventy Protestant denominations. This important step for Christian women permitted them to express their own convictions in the company of other women who shared their principles; i.e., faith in God, and faith in each other.[31] The women in the new movement were now bound together by the following intent:

- to grow in faith and extend the vision of what it means to be a Christian woman in society today.

- to become a stronger, visible, ecumenical community.

- to work for a just, peaceful, and caring society.

- to use responsibly and creatively the resources God has entrusted to us: our intelligence, time, energy, and money as we carry out the mission of Christ through Church Women United.[32]

The 1940s proved to be a very busy decade for the United Council of Church Women. In 1942, its first National Assembly was held in Cleveland, Ohio, and a national office was established at 156 Fifth Avenue in New York City.[33] The group's first major action, as noted in CWU's Souvenir Memory Book 2001, was to: "circulate a petition signed by 84,000 church women urging the United States to support the signing of the United Nations Charter, to join the organization, and to play a responsible role in such an organization. When Eleanor Roosevelt heard of the petition, she involved CWU leaders in a White House conference entitled "How Women May Share in Post-War Policy Making."[34]

Church Women United and the United Nations

From its beginnings, CWU has been a major supporter of the United Nations (UN). The women believed that the UN's organizational structure provided the means to protect women's rights and settle disputes between nations through peaceful means. In 1945, Mrs. B. Sibley attended the UN's founding meeting in San Francisco. As a member of a volunteer organization, she was invited to observe the UN's proceedings.

11

Later she would interpret the founding event to the United Council of Church Woman (UCCW) membership.[35]

In 1947, UCCW was one of the first non-government organizations to name an official observer to the United Nations.

> Mrs. Mable Head of Cleveland, Ohio, became the official observer from the UCCW to the UN. In 1948, a Mobilization for Peace Campaign distributed 1.5 million commitment cards asking women to pray for peace, support the UN, and help establish civil rights in their communities. Much later, in 1963 when the United Nations opened its Ecumenical Church Center, CWU was one of its first tenants and officially among the first non-government organizations to assign an observer with consultative status to the Department of Public Information.[36]

In 1972, the United Nations General Assembly unanimously adopted the commission's recommendation to declare 1975 International Women's Year. The International Women's Decade, 1975–1985, was also initiated at the International Women's Year Conference in Mexico City in 1975.[37]

The purpose of The International Women's Decade and the related conferences in that decade was to provide women with the opportunity to examine their governments within a world view of human rights through the United Nations' Charter. In the UN Charter gender equality is clear. Article 1 of the Charter states that: Purposes of the United Nations are to achieve international cooperation in promoting and encouraging respect for human rights and for fundamental freedoms for all, without distinction as to race, sex, language, or religion. Article II in this document further states: "Everyone is entitled to all the rights and freedoms set forth in this Declaration, without distinction of any kind, such as race, color, sex, or language."[38]

The Charter provisions offered women a framework to examine the UN's conventions related to women. It was possible to study the provisions that were in force and to determine which nations had not ratified them and why. It was also a time for women to exchange perspectives on the theme Equality, Peace, and Development, particularly in the unofficial conferences held at the same time and same place as the UN's International Women's conferences. The United Nations' Decade provided the context, and the non-governmental organizations the process, for women to discuss their common goals.

The UN's value in promoting the women's movement worldwide and incorporating the concerns of women into their programs deserves commendation. Women brought their special agendas to the Decade conferences, exchanged information, and carried their new insights back home. In a statement published in the UNITARNews for the International Women's Year 1975, Davidson Nicol, the Executive Director of the United National Institute for Training and Research, noted:

> Women, like the oppressed colonial, must in the end fight and win the struggle themselves since in doing so they not only gain strength but achieve greater self-respect and thus conquer feelings of inferiority and unworthiness which tradition imposed on them for centuries.[39]

United Council of Church Women and the National Council of Christian Churches (1950 to 1966)

In 1949, forums on women in the ecumenical church were held across the nation to prepare the United Council of Church Women (UCCW) for their role in establishing the National Council of Christian Churches. Hence, in 1950, the United Council of Church Women joined the growing movement toward church unity by becoming one of the twelve interdenominational founding organizations of the National Council of Christian Churches (NCCC) in the USA located in New York City."[40] The women felt they could better implement their missionary work and be fully integrated into the life of the church by joining the NCCC. As a department of the NCCC, the United Council of Church Women was promised certain safeguards:

- the retention of their right to organize, develop, and serve local and state councils of church women
- the right to call a national assembly
- the right to review work and set goals
- the right of local and state councils to select their own officers
- the autonomy to manage their own finances
- the right to protect its political power in the proposed new body and its presence in the larger world
- the assurance of representation on the governing board and the executive committee, and the recognition of its name must be conserved, not by absorption or amalgamation, but through diversity.[41]

After the merger, the women were known as the General Department of United Church Women of the National Council of Churches of Christ.[42]

In less than two decades, however, the relationship between UCW and the NCCC fell apart, due to broken promises. The women were given very little control over the money they were raising, and the NCCC refused to allow the local UCW to include an increasing number of denominations that were not member churches of the NCCC. For example, among other violations, UCW was not allowed to increase the participation of Roman Catholics and Greek Orthodox women.[43] As a result, in the mid-1960s separation from the NCCC became inevitable. After a progression of name changes, by 1970 UCW became Church Women United and an independent movement.[44] The women emphasized the need to demonstrate their unity and take action together.

16

CHAPTER TWO

CHURCH WOMEN UNITED: STRUCTURE AND GOVERNANCE

Church Women United created a network of components unique to its mission and goals. The women saw themselves within the larger human sphere and committed to a circle where access to one another is always possible.

> Church Women United was formed around a practice of circularity: worship, study, prayer, celebration, and action. When CWU identified those as its context of involvement, it envisioned them not as stages of a linear journey but in a circular configuration: no starting point, no ending; one grows out of another, derives strength from another, and gives strength to another such as how the local, state, and national units of CWU interact. There is constant movement for good....[45]

The structure of national Church Women United, includes Common Council, the National Action and Global Committee, the National Assembly, regional coordinators, and state and local units. According to the CWU national By-laws,

> Common Council is the highest legislative authority of Church Women United, Inc., and shall deal with all matters which are necessary in pursuit of the purpose and functions of this organization" (Article V Section 1); the National Action and Global Committee monitors global and national issues and develops social policy statements for the Board of Directors approval. Once approved, the committee interprets the

17

statements and applies them to specific social issues by developing policies, resolutions, recommendations, and statements of concern, which become the basis for CWU programs and social advocacy.[46]

Every four years the Common Council assembles to ratify CWU resolutions, policies, and public statements. During this assembly, quadrennial priorities are voted on. These range in scope from local to global human needs. Once the priorities are adopted, the agenda for the movement's social advocacy is set for the next four years and guides CWU's work in the national, state, and local units.[47] The priorities are as follows:

Bringing God's Shalom/Salaam to our World: Church Women United's Quadrennial Priority for 2012–2016

Health: Promote the health and well being of all people.

> 1 Corinthians 6:19–20. What? Know ye not that your body is the temple of the Holy Ghost which is in you, which ye have of God, and ye are not your own? For ye are bought with a price: therefore, glorify God in your body, and in your spirit, which are God's.

Environmental Care: Promote personal, communal, and governmental decisions that express care for all.

> Psalms 96:11–13. Let the heavens rejoice and let the earth be glad; let the sea roar, and the fullness thereof. Let the field be joyful, and all that is therein: then shall all the trees of the woods rejoice before the Lord: for he cometh to judge the earth: he shall judge the world with righteousness, and the people with his truth.

Justice: Promote shalom through understanding, education, confession, forgiveness, reconciliation and non-violence.

> Micah 6:8. He hath shewed thee, O man, what is good; and what doth the Lord require of thee, but to do justly, and to love mercy, and to walk humbly with thy God?

Economic Justice: Promote the dignity, safety, and economic opportunities for all people.

> Isaiah 58: 6–10. Is not this the fast that I have chosen? To loose the bands of wickedness, to undo the heavy burdens, and to let the oppressed go free, and that ye break every yoke? Is it not to deal thy bread to the hungry, and that thou bring the poor that are cast out to thy house? When thou seest the naked that thou cover him, and that thou hide not thyself from thine own flesh? Then shall thy light break forth as the morning, and thine health shall spring forth speedily: and thy righteousness shall go before thee; the glory of the Lord shall be thy reward. Then shalt thou call, and the Lord shall answer; thou shall cry and he shall say, Here I am. If thou take away from the midst of thee the yoke, the putting forth of the finger, and speaking vanity; And if thou draw out thy soul to the hungry and satisfy the afflicted soul; then shall thy light rise in obscurity, and thy darkness be as the noon day.

Washington/Northern Idaho State Unit

According to Alice Hoaglund, historian and former president of the Washington/Northern Idaho state unit, the very earliest beginnings of the Washington State unit date back to 1936 when a State Council of Church Woman (Protestant) was formed in response to needs among migrant workers. The original communities were Spokane, Seattle, Tacoma, Longview, Yakima, and Bremerton. Thousands of migrants entered the state of Washington each year, most from Texas and California. They were at the bottom of the economic ladder and subject to exploitation. They needed the service of the Christian community and received it from the State Council of Church Women.

In the 1940s the Stamp Project began through the efforts of Dr. Gertrude Apel of the Seattle Council of Churches. This project, which developed funds from used stamps, contributed such funds to Church World Service. It was during this decade that the Washington State unit bonded with the northern Idaho unit. The event coincided with the national formation of United Church Women in 1941. The 1960s found the state participating actively in the "Assignment Race" emphasis.

Marion Malonson of Seattle became the first Roman Catholic state president in the 1970s. With the nuclear build-up and the Cold War going on in the 1980s, the state participated in the Peace Ribbon project. Jan Cate of Seattle was one of the leaders promoting the project, and almost every unit produced at least one part of the ten-mile ribbon that surrounded the Pentagon. Also, in the 1980s, the Washington State unit elected its first African American woman, Mary Golden of Bremerton, to serve as state president.

In November of 1981, John Spellman, the Governor of Washington, proclaimed the week of December 6 through December 12 as Church Women United Week. This was no doubt an outgrowth of the 40th anniversary of the founding of national CWU. In the governor's proclamation, Spellman wrote of this "outstanding organization...whose members have labored diligently as advocates for the rights of the poor, the elderly, the handicapped, and the disadvantaged."

Over the years state assemblies have hosted visiting national leadership. Among them national presidents; Claire Collins Harvey, Thelma Adair, Sylvia Talbot, Claire Randall, and Ann Garvin. Each has contributed richly to the state movement, which continues to advocate for those in need today. State units serve the local units within its jurisdiction not only as a resource, but also as an initiator of action and communications.

A State Leaders Council meets annually to receive unit reports, explore issues of concern to Christian women, formulate recommendations to the state board to direct units, exchange information, provide orientation and leadership development, and approve any statement to be issued in the name of CWU.

Each unit operates for the sake of the whole movement and is an important part of the national movement because it shares the:

- mission, common goals and quadrennial priorities
- national program
- national publications and publicity
- national office and staff
- financial resources

Local Units

At one point, Church Women United was comprised of 1,200 local units throughout the United States and Puerto Rico. Today, in 2014, there are eight hundred active local units. CWU is organized according to separate by-laws in each local community. "The term *unit* was adopted to define a local, state, or regional area that has operated under its own by-laws, but was in harmony with the national purpose. Each unit also develops its own organizational style and program within the national framework, spirit, mission, and common goals of Church Women United." [48] National CWU is in the process of updating the definition of a CWU unit. At present, four options are offered to church women who desire to become a CWU unit: "Option 1)

21

CWU Local Unit; Option 2) Celebrations Unit; Option 3) World Day of Prayer Unit; Option 4)" CWU Affiliate Unit (see Appendix A).

CHAPTER THREE

THE HISTORICAL, RELIGIOUS, AND SOCIAL CULTURE OF CHURCH WOMEN UNITED

Women in the movement always knew that prayer alone was not sufficient to right wrongs, and neither were statements—no matter how highly principled. Church Women United (CWU) leaders had specifically emphasized this in 1955 when they urged members to become more active and take more responsibility in civic and political life. CWU believes this to be an important part of Christian responsibility.

As women of faith, CWU has persisted in its united witness through study, prayer, peace-seeking, and advocating for justice. Its religious, spiritual, and cultural elements are uniquely interwoven within its social justice advocacy and celebrations. CWU's policy statements, resolutions, and quadrennial priorities have enabled women in the organization to respond to numerous national and international issues from the 1960s to 2014. Examples of CWU's advocacy began with the United States' involvement in Indo-China.

1960–1969

As a peace promoter, the CWU movement has called for conflicts to be settled through negotiations, not by arms. During this period, however, challenges to societal values were manifested in social reform efforts and by counter-cultural movements. For example, due to America's involvement in the Vietnam War and the bombing of Cambodia (1964 to 1972), the greatest anti-war movement the nation had ever experienced developed in the United States. In addition to participating in marches against the Vietnam War, CWU voted to adopt the following Statement of Concern (1971) for America's continuing involvement in Indochina.

We cannot accept the system which substitutes Asian casualties for Americans and provides people with weapons to kill their own. We call upon church women to persuade our government to end this war through complete United States withdrawal."[49]

Anti-Racism and Civil Rights

Working for civil rights, racial justice, and equality have been on the agenda for CWU since its earliest days. For example, anti-racism and civil rights actions became national CWU programs. Beginning in 1960, an initiative called 'Assignment Race' gained national attention through two significant articles in the *Christian Century*. The first article, noted here, was entitled "U.C.W. to Campaign Against Racism":

United Church Women at its Ninth National Assembly in Miami Beach, Florida, courageously launched a nationwide, inter-denominational attack on racial discrimination in churches, housing, schools and places of employment. The program, Assignment Race, 1961–1964, approved by the board of managers of UCW, invited 12 million Protestant and Orthodox churchwomen in 35 denominations to join in breaking down racial barriers. UCW has consistently exhibited a pioneering spirit in confronting the social issues of our time with the Christian ethic. In this instance, UCW merits the salute which it received from President Kennedy when its Ninth Assembly opened. Kennedy said, 'the work of United Church Women on the new frontiers of human rights, economic growth and universal education, at home and in other parts of the world, has become increasingly important in these

24

days of tension and crisis. Your enlightened and constructive leadership is a vital contribution to World peace and progress.'[50]

The second article published was entitled "Church Women Lay Faith on the Line":

Over the next three years churchwomen in this country will be laying their Christian faith on the line in a concerted attempt to commit the church to racial justice. Under the leadership of United Church Women, a pledge is being circulated. Signers commit themselves to witness to the kingship of Christ and to work for the unity of all mankind through social and political action. While this is no bandwagon movement, Assignment Race is, in our opinion, one of the most significant expressions of Practical Christianity originating in American churches in the past 15 years.[51]

In response to the initiative, CWU regional meetings took place throughout the country. Negro and white women became aware that one of the greatest supports to an individual's effort to eliminate racism was associating with others who were making the same effort.[52] Nevertheless, in the long run, the value of Assignment Race may well have not been what UCW contributed to human rights as much as what happened in the constituency of UCW itself. A widespread program of leadership training of peers was carried out by means of interracial teams, which proved valuable. CWU had its own response to the growing civil rights movement as Margaret Shannon remarked:

The women considered the Civil Rights Movement of the 60s as birth pangs of hope for our nation; hope for the inalienable rights of many black citizens; hope for a truly multi-racial society for the benefit of us all; hope for spiritual renewal among Christians and Jews together in the crucible where our claims for a God of justice were being tested.[53]

In the U.S., members of CWU held leadership roles in marches and worked behind the scenes during the civil rights movement. The women of CWU firmly upheld the protections reflected in the Bill of Rights and asserted that they be applied equally to all citizens. Most importantly, they sought full implementation for all of the First Amendment (1791) to the U.S. Constitution which promises "protection for the rights of citizens to assemble in groups, hold demonstrations and meetings in support of their beliefs, and to petition the government for a redress of grievances."[54]

Unfortunately, the dissenters' right to hold demonstrations throughout the south was often violated. For example, in Albany, Georgia, in the 1960s, mass demonstrations took place and thousands went to jail for assembling and marching to protest racism and segregation in America. In Birmingham, Alabama, African Americans faced police clubs, tear gas, dogs, and high-powered water hoses. The Department of Justice recorded 1,412 demonstrations in the first three months of 1963.[55]

In support of the demonstrators' efforts, CWU voted to endorse a statement called The Right to Dissent, which was adopted by the General Board of the NCCC, on February 22, 1966. Consequently, when the women responded to the call to work for peace with justice, they found themselves in the forefront of working to eradicate racism in America.

Nevertheless, African Americans soon realized that, in spite of the passage of the 1965 Voting Rights Act outlawing discrimination in voting, their plight was unchanged. Voting was important, but at that time, it did not solve the issue of racism and poverty. During no period of the twentieth century were

African Americans free from the struggle against injustices and the inconsistencies of American democracy—which continues today. Therefore, the civil rights movement of the 60s and 70s was simply a continuation of the socio-political struggles of previous years due to persistent discrimination and segregation in employment, education, and housing.

Populations of impoverished African Americans were concentrated in major cities where racial tensions increased:

> Between 1964 and 1968, race riots shattered many American cities, with federal troops deployed in the Watts Riots in Los Angeles as well as in the Detroit and Washington, D.C., riots. In Memphis, Tennessee, in the summer of 1968, Civil Rights leader, Reverend Martin Luther King, Jr. was murdered by an assassin. There were many new civil disturbances in many cities but some immediate good came from this tragedy: a bill outlawing racial discrimination in housing had been languishing in Congress. King's murder renewed momentum for the measure. With President Johnson determined to see it pass, Congress yielded to his will and passed the Civil Rights Act of 1968. The resulting law began to open up the suburbs to minority residents, though it would be several decades before segregated housing patterns would be improved.[56]

Re-Assignment Race

Women in CWU were disappointed by the lack of progress against racism; therefore, in 1981, a proclamation against racism was re-issued by CWU National President Dr. Thelma Adair, An African American Presbyterian minister. She wrote:

> Church Women United, rejoicing in God's gift of diversity and celebrating the infinite worth of each person created in God's image and loved by Jesus Christ, deplores the malignant resurgence of racism in our society. Empowered by God's Spirit, we renew our commitment to work for the elimination of the root causes of racism and for all human dignity, liberty, equality and justice for all people.[57]

Adair's proclamation resulted in a second national program emphasis called Re-Assignment: Race. Local units throughout the nation presented consciousness-raising and skill-building workshops to counteract this resurgence of racism. The SCWU unit, for example, under the leadership of President Jeraldine Bright, CWU activist Annie Jones, and supporters Dolores Jones, Gloria Thompson, and others who were committed to the mission, held forums focused on racial stereotypes and conducted an internal assessment of its membership.

Concerns for the equal treatment of women became another priority for CWU during this period. In 1969, the national officers of CWU created the Commission on Women in Today's World. Its functions included:

> Identifying the primary issues that concern the full participation of woman as a person in church and society; gathering relevant data and current information on developments to be shared with the national denominational leadership; and

making recommendations for action that enables church women to utilize their power to achieve full and responsible positions in both church and society.[58]

1970–1979

Values struggles that emerged in many main-line denominations impacted CWU. Conservative groups focused on patriotism, patriarchs, narrow theological understandings, and anti-ecumenism.[59] Nevertheless, in 1972, CWU brought emerging women theologians and lay women, who were involved in the women's movement, into the churches. This created opportunities for women as full participants in church life. Also, in Michigan in 1972 and in Oklahoma in 1973, CWU took action regarding the lack of women in church policy-making. CWU convened a workshop, "Women in Church Government" for women members of boards where there were male majorities.

A dozen major denominational agencies selected the women participants. At the work-shops, the participants helped each other to realize their place and their power in mixed company where male dominance for over a hundred years had established an approved process. They discussed their own role in this transition period, awaiting the time to come when both men and women would more nearly understand each other's gifts and accept them.[60]

Early in 1970, when Church Women United became aware of the need to develop a common platform on pluralism—because of the increasing racial and ethnic populations in America—they issued a communication on "Living Together in a Pluralistic Society." The communication stated:

29

Church Women United affirms its commitment to live according to our God-given conviction of the worth of each individual and recognizes that our unity as a nation depends upon our ability to work together in a society and to discover the cultural contributions coming from every race and nation.[61]

By 1976, The People's Platform for a Global Society evolved from a CWU-initiated study:

In the years preceding the nation's bicentennial (1976) Church Women United in every state studied their society and wrote a platform for action called The Peoples Platform for a Global Society. The resulting document was formed into planks that were from hundreds of local units writing about problems of society and the principles to address them. The scriptural theme was the gospel admonition 'As you did it to one of the least of these my little ones, you did it unto me' (Matt. 25). Church Women United's Peoples Platform for a Global Society: Mandate for Action, was presented to newly-elected President Jimmy Carter.[62]

To remove the obstacles and barriers that prevented and hindered women's equal status in society, a movement for equal rights for women was also part of the political and social landscape of America during the 1970s and 1980s. Women did not receive equal pay for equal work in spite of Title VII of the 1964 Civil Rights Act, which prohibited job discrimination on the basis of sex and race.[63]

A proposed amendment designed to guarantee equal rights for women was approved by Congress in 1972 and sent to the states for ratification. In 1975, CWU convened a Religious

30

Committee on the Equal Rights Amendment (ERA). The women worked hard to influence state legislators and Congress to support the amendment—a simple twenty-four-word sentence: "Equality of rights under the law shall not be denied or abridged by the United States or by any State on account of sex."[64] In spite of the efforts of CWU and many others, "by 1977 only thirty-five states, three short of the necessary thirty-eight, had approved the amendment. Congress extended the deadline for ratification to June 30, 1982, but no additional states ratified the amendment. The ERA was defeated."[65]

1980–1989

Distrust of America's political system

As time went on, a culture of distrust in America's political system flooded the country. The historic resignation of President Richard Nixon in August 1974 caused many Americans to refuse to identify themselves as either Democrats or Republicans. "In 1974, 34% of registered voters identified themselves as independent."[66] Economic insecurity was also a concern. Dissatisfaction grew because of economic inflation and unemployment, which had increased since 1973. There was a significant decline in hope and confidence that things would get better.

The election of President Jimmy Carter represented an attempt by the Democratic Party to recapture a disillusioned citizenry, but the strategy failed. For example, as one writer noted, "While the poor were taking cuts, the salary of the chairman of Exxon Oil was being raised to $830,000 a year."[67] Increased poverty throughout the nation spurred CWU members to write their legislators and congressmen to urge them to enact legislation to end hunger and homelessness.

In 1984, National CWU opened an office in Washington, D.C. to further strengthen CWU's ecumenical witness. The office was created to *equip* women of faith to become informed advocates for change, and later to *inform* CWU constituents through a quarterly on-line newsletter called "Inform and Act." The D.C. office also sent out alerts on timely issues and lobbying events on Capitol Hill.

CWU's team at the D.C. office advocates directly to the U.S. Congress through letter writing, petitions, and meetings with congressional and White House staff. Presently, Stephanie Jones is the Advocacy Coordinator for CWU. Ms. Jones monitors and supports measures consistent with CWU's Quadrennial Priorities, social policies, and resolutions. She also clarifies the moral issues at stake in public policies, while expressing those concerns to the appropriate person in agencies that have policies our government supports.

During this period, many Latino and Latina activists organized around specific issues, such as Bilingual Education in the schools, tenant laws, and improved labor conditions. These efforts were designed to increase fairness and level the playing field for all Americans.[68]

CWU's goal was to make their opposition to war known so it responded to issues regarding nuclear armaments and the threat of a nuclear war. In 1980 one of CWU's many activities was advocacy for a freeze on nuclear weapons. It was voted, by CWU's national board of directors, that the national President send a letter to the President of the United States to protest production, testing, and the deployment of nuclear weapons.

In one instance, some members of CWU took direct action to emphasize the gravity of the situation. Realizing that North Dakota was the third largest nuclear power in the world, Sister Marjorie Tuite, CWU's Social Action Director, and twenty-eight women with peace and justice as their motto, organized a peace bus tour of the state in 1983.[69]

Meanwhile, Corporate America benefited from both the Reagan and Bush administrations as poverty continued to increase. "In 1982, thirty million people were unemployed. Millions of Americans lost medical insurance, which was tied to their job."[70]

By the end of President Reagan's term, the gap between the rich and the poor in the United States was widened. African Americans were hit hard as were women, Hispanics, and Native-Americans. "At the end of the 1980s thousands of families fell below the poverty line. The economic and social crisis the nation faced was primarily rooted in economic and social structures that made it impossible for the poor to afford basic human needs."[71] CWU believed that constant monitoring was necessary to protect the impoverished. They issued the following statement:

> The theological basis for CWU's statement on hunger was that: all people are created equal and called in covenant (Gen. 9:13) to continue to share in the work of creation by imaging God's love and care . . . God's intention, therefore, is that all people's dignity is to be preserved and that all people have access to the resources they need to live in dignity.[72]

Additionally, in 1988, because of deep concerns with the poverty of women and children, CWU launched a major Campaign to End Hunger and Homelessness.

1990–2000

Immigration Challenges

Immigration challenged the religious and social culture of America as each wave of immigrants brought the religions of the world to America. People from these religions often united because of their religious values. Their cooperative efforts led to the creation of new religious denominations, such as the United Church of Christ, as well as inter-church agencies, such as the National Association of Evangelicals.[73] International unrest, however, created conflict that challenged local and national tolerance.

Moreover, during the Clinton administration (1993–2001), economic problems arising from the recession inflamed anti-immigrant feelings. Americans feared that the nation was losing control of its borders. They were also still worried about the long-term prospects for the economy. These attitudes influenced political action. "In 1993 President Clinton announced his determination to crack down on illegal immigration, but in spite of new legislation, such as the Immigration Reform and Control Act (IRCA), the estimated number of illegal aliens rose to between two to four million by 1993."[74] CWU's basis for involvement in the immigration issue was based on the following scriptures:

> The stranger that dwells among you shall be unto you as one born among you, and you shall love him as yourself. . . (Exodus 12:48); I was a stranger and you took me in. . . (Matt. 25:35); Be not forgetful to entertain strangers for thereby some have entertained angels unawares (Hebrews 13:2).

During various periods CWU has responded to immigration issues. In the 1970s, CWU joined with other organizations in requesting that the national government initiate an immigration policy to address the following areas: differential immigration classifications, the human rights of all aliens, cultural orientation, and delivery of services. The immigration problem remained, however, and in 1981, CWU issued another policy statement:

> Large numbers of persons residing in the United States are classified as undocumented and over-stayed. Because we place a strong emphasis on the family, we believe family reunification should be protected in our immigration law. We also believe the United States Government should grant political asylum to all refugees fleeing persecution, and we affirm the right of all people to education, medical, and social services, without regard to citizenship or legal status. Historically, CWU has called on its constituency to participate in the resettlement of immigrants and refugees. We affirm this and call on CWU to continue this ministry.[75]

Economic justice was also a major issue. Under President Clinton, the North American Free Trade Agreement (NAFTA) with Mexico was passed. "The agreement removed obstacles to corporate capital and goods moving back and forth across the Mexican-U.S. border without restriction."[76] CWU responded to this trade agreement with a Statement of Concern adopted by the CWU's Executive Council on March 21, 1999. Issued from Atlanta, Georgia, the statement reads as follows:

> We are concerned about the North American Free Trade Agreement (NAFTA). The side agreements on labor and the environment do not provide real enforcements mechanisms. NAFTA contributes to globalization that does not strengthen com-

munities. As women of faith, we are committed to building relationships of economic and social justice for all people of this hemisphere. Therefore, we oppose this NAFTA treaty and urge Church Women United to contact their members of Congress to express their concern. We will continue, however, to work towards trade agreements based on the principles of fairness and equity.[77]

Other problems during this decade led to American citizens' dissatisfaction. While types of violence are distinct, one form of violence can lead to another creating a downward destructive cycle. During this period, for example, crime and violence were often associated with the drug trade, which moved out from the inner cities into the suburbs and rural areas. Dissatisfaction with public education also increased during the Clinton Administration as schools dealt with more disruptive behaviors as scholastic achievement declined. The drop-out rate also escalated.

In the 1990s American schools were characterized as the least successful in the industrial world. "Only 30 percent of adult Americans earned a high school diploma and only 13.1 percent were graduates of a four-year college."[78] Thus, educational reform efforts began. Public Charter Schools became independent of states and gained ground. Private business firms were also contracted to manage many public schools. Some programs even allowed parents to use tax-exempt vouchers to send their children to private or Parochial Schools.[79] Many of the reform efforts were successful and some were not, mainly because public charter schools were often perceived as an opportunity for private schools to be established with public money. Nevertheless, Church Women United advocated for effective, accessible education, quality schools for all children, education for parenthood, adult education, literacy, and pre-school needs of children.

2000–2010

In 2003, CWU agreed to support a Young Church Women Initiative focused on involving younger women (from ages 21 to 45) in CWU and likewise supporting them on their faith journey. CWU's hope was to revitalize the movement. According to CWU, the Initiative is an ongoing process designed to spread across all CWU regions by the Young Church Women United Initiative Team. The initiative is still an active force within CWU, and is being implemented, but no official report has been released detailing its success.[80]

War and Rumors of Wars

A major issue of this decade proved to be the Iraq War. In the streets of major American cities pro-war groups clashed with those who opposed the war. CWU's Common Council passed a resolution in 2008 asking the president of the United States to renew efforts to end the war along with creating a timeline for U.S. troop withdrawal. Individual CWU members were encouraged to continue to be in contact with their congressional representatives to change the course of the Iraq War.[81]

The Middle East became a major focus of American foreign policy and a priority for CWU. "The 1948 United Nations Declaration that 55% of Palestine would be known as Israel was intended to provide a good solution for Jewish refugees and those fleeing persecution. Instead, 700,000 Palestinians were displaced from their homes and became refugees; this group increased to three million."[82] The ongoing difficulties between Israel and its Arab neighbors intensified when Israel became an armed camp with security check points for Arabs. Warfare led to Arab imprisonment and lost lives.

In 2008, CWU strongly urged the United States government, along with representatives of Israel, Palestine, neighboring Arab countries, the European Union, and the United Nations to meet and negotiate a cease-fire. The CWU Resolution stated the following:

> During the negotiation period, there will be the following accomplishments: U.S. aid to build housing settlements for Palestinians in the areas outside the West Bank, Gaza, and East Jerusalem; any further military aid to Israel would be halted until this was accomplished; U.S. funding would help Israelis in their move to the new settlements as well as provide for the Palestinians resettling in the vacated houses; rebuild homes destroyed by Israeli use of our military aid, and replant Palestinian farms and orchards destroyed during the fighting.[83]

Despite CWU's efforts, nothing was accomplished during this negotiation period. The ongoing struggle for a homeland for the Palestinians has escalated over the years.

In 2006, CWU again addressed U.S. immigration issues. CWU's National Board of Directors endorsed the following interfaith statement in support of comprehensive immigration reform. The statement included reasonable criteria for a lawful permanent residence and eventual citizenship:

- reform of the government's family-based immigration system
- policies that allow workers and their families to enter the U.S. and work in a legal, safe and orderly manner
- border protection practices that are consistent with humanitarian values while preventing entry of dangerous criminals and terrorists.

The Board commended the statement to both state and local units for study and action (Adopted by CWU's Board of Directors 2005). Although the immigration issue has not been resolved by Congress, CWU on both the national and local levels continue to monitor this issue.

The elimination of discrimination against women was a long-standing priority with CWU. In 2010, CWU adopted a resolution that "urged the President of the United States to transmit the United Nations Convention on the Elimination of All Forms of Discrimination Against Women (CEDAW) to the United States Senate, seeking its consent to undertake the process of the CEDAW's ratification" (Resolution in Support of CEDAW approved by the Executive Council of Church Women United on April 8, 2010).

CHAPTER FOUR

CHURCH WOMEN UNITED AND ECUMENISM

Ecumenism, one of the foundational principles of Church Women United (CWU), reflects the universality of God's plan for humankind. As the foundation of its ecumenical witness, CWU pursues unity, love, justice, peace, and faith in Jesus Christ. CWU has adhered to an official tenet of ecumenism found in Jesus' prayer to God in the Garden of Gethsemane, "that they may be one, as we are one" (John 17:11). Consequently, over the years, CWU has accepted that scripture as having historical importance to the movement as well as having contemporary relevance.

Two interesting interpretations of ecumenism (among many) were written about in *The Church Woman*. Former national UCW President Cynthia Wydel, described ecumenism as "the coming back together of the scattered family of God." The other description by Margaret Shannon, CWU lay historian and former Executive Director, indicated that there was a sense of understanding by church women that. . .

> Ecumenism was an experience, a movement in which women could initiate programs of corporate significance, [and] prove that [they] could mobilize an affirmative response to the challenges of the times and bear the pain and changes of a world in turmoil).[84]

Aligned with that understanding, Margaret Shannon also held

> That the purpose of CWU is to encourage church women to come together in a visible fellowship to witness to their faith in Jesus Christ and, enabled by the Holy Spirit, to go out together into every

41

neighborhood and nation as instruments of reconciling love in pursuit of peace and justice as the foundation for authentic witness to Christ. Comprised of Christian church women, the local movement spread itself statewide, nationwide, and later worldwide, demonstrating and witnessing to unity in Christ.[85]

Ecumenism and the Church

The roots of the Christian Ecumenical Movement evolved from the historic 1910 World Missionary Conference in Edinburgh, Scotland. The conference focused on the Church and its Witness."[86] However, the unity of Christian witness remains incomplete for several reasons. Ecumenical groups have struggled for years to overcome differences in the particularities of faith traditions, doctrinal conflicts, cultural and racial diversity, economic disparity, and in some cases, political oppression. These challenges confront both the World Council of Churches (WCC) and the National Council of Christian Churches (NCCC), the two primary ecumenical bodies through which mainstream Protestant denominations have participated.[87]

The WCC ecumenical movement has sought to unite Christian Churches throughout the world. For example, Christian leaders from churches in Asia, Africa, Europe, Latin America, Canada, South America, the United States, and the Caribbean met throughout the twentieth century and continue to meet during the twenty-first century. Moreover, because variations within Christian denominations are found within the nations of the world, assemblies such as the First Assembly of the All-African Conference of Churches and the European Ecumenical Assembly also hold meetings.[88]

Changes in the philosophical and theological underpinnings of ecumenism have also created conflicts. The first two phases of the movement were strongly Christocentric, as indicated by the WCC's foundational statement that it is a fellowship of churches which confess the Lord Jesus Christ as God and Savior according to the scriptures. The focus was also on the church as the universal body of Christ. The mission was seen as the proclamation of Christ throughout the world emphasizing the Divinity of Christ, which was thought to be crucial at a time when human society was disordered by global conflict.[89]

A shift occurred, however, that emphasized the Trinitarian nature of God, the Spirit's sustaining presence throughout creation, the humanity of Christ, and his suffering in solidarity with those who lived on the margins of history. During the final phase of the twentieth century, the movement focused on such things as sharing, healing, and participation.[90]

William B. Cate, PhD., former Executive Director of the Church Council of Greater Seattle, noted that a fresh perspective on the unity of local churches in America was a priority:

> We need fresh thinking to envision the unity we seek as Christians in America today. How can the churches more fully manifest their unity and become effective agents of God's kingdom of peace, love and justice in our communities? The focus of ecumenical energy is to be found in a new understanding of the local church and the envisioning of a unity which is primarily local. With a new focus on the local church as a new theology of Ecumenism, each tradition is to preserve and share, but the denominational tradition would not be the important vehicle for mobilization of the church for mission in the world. The local church in the Seattle area, for example, would be integrated racially, although there could be varied fellowships of African

43

American, Caucasian, or Asian churches. These separate fellowships would still be an integral part of the one local Church of Greater Seattle; local Christians in one place centered around our loyalty to Jesus Christ.[91]

The World Council of Churches also seeks to bring visible unity to the Universal Church of God through dialogue that offers an opportunity for Christian witness. For example, the document of *Baptism, Eucharist, and Ministry* was produced by the WCC's Commission on Faith and Order.[92] It represented a new level of theological convergence on crucial issues that were prerequisites to reconciliation. Active participation by the Roman Catholics began with the Second Vatican Council (1962 to 1965) when Catholic, Protestant, and Orthodox Christians made common witness in various areas of the world through genuine partnership.[93]

Bilateral conversations between Roman Catholics and Lutherans have resulted in once unthinkable consensus on such matters as Justification by Faith, the Work of the *Triune God: God the Father, His Son Jesus Christ, the Holy Spirit*, and Grace, the gift of God through Jesus Christ. These agreements are both aspects of the Christian Joint Declaration on the Doctrine of Justification.[94]

Women's Participation

Women's participation at the first assembly of the WCC in Amsterdam, Netherlands, August 22, to September 4, 1948, was a significant historic event but was limited in terms of the number of women present and their actual contribution to the debates and decisions. Nevertheless, a study on the Life and Work of Women in the Church was commissioned by the Faith and Order Commission. When the women met, the attendees were highly competent and experienced church women. It was evident that the ordination of women was a sensitive ecumenical issue and was raised in the context of the inquiry by the committee on the Life and Work of Women in the church, even though it was seen as only a minor part of the whole problem. Women insisted that the question of women's place in the church was a theological and ecclesiological issue; it had to do with the very nature of the Church and with their membership in the Body of Christ.[95] Their report regarding this issue began with a brief theological statement: "The Church as the body of Christ consists of men and women created, as responsible persons, together to glorify God and to do His will."[96]

Progress was made in Amsterdam, Netherlands, where the foundation was laid for greater future participation of women. A movement began, which continued throughout successive assemblies and within the ongoing life of the WCC, towards the full equality of women with men. The progress made is evidenced by the following: in Amsterdam in 1948, out of 351 delegates, 5.7 percent were women; in Evanston, Illinois, in 1954, out of 502 delegates, 8.5 percent were women; in New Delhi, India, in1961, out of 577 delegates, 7.2 percent were women; in Uppsala, Sweden in 1968, out of 704 delegates, 9 percent were women. When the Assembly was held in Nairobi, Kenya, in 1975, out of 676 delegates, 22 percent were women; in Vancouver, British Columbia, Canada in 1983, out of 847 delegates from the WCC member churches 29.49 percent were women and in Canberra in 1991, out of 842 present, 35 percent were women. Each day more than 4,500 people attended the Assembly.[97]

In Vancouver, British Columbia in 1983, the theme was "Jesus Christ—The Life of the World." During this time, there was a resurgence of militarization, an economic crisis, and the growing awareness of the ecological crisis and its relationship to the gap between First and Third World countries.[98]

Women contributed significantly to a number of the plenary presentations in the nature of "testimonies," and made powerful statements about their struggles and concerns as women and human beings. A theological presentation on the sub-theme Life in its Fullness was made by German theologian Dorothee Solle. Pauline Webb, Moderator of the Assembly planning committee, broke new ground when she preached the sermon at the opening worship on "The Word of Life." Overall, from the opening act of worship, women participated actively in the worship life of the Assembly. It was there that many stereotypical attitudes against women's spiritual leadership were broken down. Both men and women shared in the events that included preaching, praying, singing, symbolic action, and the Eucharist.

As noted earlier, at the 1991 Assembly held in Canberra, Australia, out of 842 delegates, 35 percent were women. At the 2013 Tenth Assembly, which was held in Bussan, South Korea, Dr. Agnes Abuom, an African woman from Nairobi, Kenya, became Moderator of the highest World Council of Churches governing body.

While the WCC and the NCCC are movements primarily driven by committed individuals, ecumenism is the work of organizations and councils led by official Church representatives. The ecumenical focus is also on the unity and renewal of the Church as a sign and instrument of God's intention for the world; i.e., renewal of the world of which the Church is a part, and unity as a gift of God that needs only to be claimed. This is a calling by which the movement thrives. The failure of churches to demonstrate this unity to the world concerns many ecumenists who believe the following:

> What the world does not see in the all too visible disunity of the churches is a sign that the Word became flesh and dwelt among us, full of grace and truth (John 1:1). What the disunity of the

churches obscures is God's glory as of the only Son from the Father (John 1:14, RSV). Therefore, the credibility of the Gospel (John 3:16) depends upon the unity of the church by which that life is exhibited to the world. The unity of the church, therefore, is a necessary condition for holding the Gospel true. Thus, the call for Christian unity is not for the sake of the churches but for the sake of the world.[99]

Further, during a recent interview, Reverend James Forbes, Senior Pastor Emeritus of the Riverside Church in New York City, said "If the church is truly to be a church, a healing of the spirit is needed. In spite of the fact that some barriers to unity have been reduced, there is not a functional organization to promote the unity of God's children and the inclusiveness of God's love."[100]

CHAPTER FIVE

SEATTLE CHURCH WOMEN UNITED

This Chapter provides background on the history of Seattle Church Women United (SCWU), its relationship to both national and state units, and its social justice praxis and programs from its beginnings. Eloise Boulding's book, the *Underside of History*, reminds us that often the work of Christian women down through the centuries has been unrecorded and hence forgotten.[101] Unfortunately, this is the situation of the Seattle Church Women United unit. Overall, very little attention was given to maintaining minutes, preserving important documents, or archiving the unit's history. Fortunately, the Church Council of Greater Seattle (CCGS) retained, and shared with the author, SCWU historical articles that had been published in the "Women and Religion" section of the Church Council's publication *The Source*. The articles offer important information about the activities of SCWU during the 1980s, but sadly nothing beyond that decade.

Equally important for discussing SCWU's history, was an unfinished manuscript entitled "Church Women United in the Seattle Area" compiled and written by Mrs. Jessie Kinnear Kenton, a Presbyterian historian and former executive administrator for the Church Council of Greater Seattle.

The prologue of Mrs. Kenton's manuscript offers the following:

> Much of the information contained in the manuscript was secured while researching Changing Values in Ecumenical Work in the Greater Seattle Area from 1919 to 1984, a thesis prepared in 1985 as a part of the requirements for

49

a Masters Degree from the San Francisco Theological Seminary.[102]

Mrs. Kenton is a credible source, and some of her information has proved valuable in preparing this chapter.

The Early History of Church Women United

A study of nineteenth-century church history in the Seattle area indicates that the characteristic pattern of religious cooperation tended to be nondenominational and unofficial. Church people worked to further a variety of good causes and necessary reforms. "Although we know local women were working cooperatively in Sunday Schools and in Mission work, the first record of a Seattle President of Church Women is in 1923. Mrs. S. D. Wingate served as President of Church Women until December 1924."[103]

According to Mrs. Kenton, there was no mention of a previous group called "Church Women" in the Seattle area. In 1925 Bertha K. Landis, the first and, to date, only woman elected to serve as Mayor of Seattle, urged women to get involved in civic work. It was not until 1942, however, that church women were asked to help register voters.

The Reverend Gertrude Apel made many advances on behalf of church women and ecumenism from the 1930s through the 1960s. As General Secretary, she forged the Washington-Northern Idaho and Seattle Councils of Churches and Christian Education into one of the most noteworthy ecumenical agencies in the nation. In her concluding years, she undertook a career as founding pastor of the suburban Marine View Methodist Church in Federal Way, located between Seattle and Tacoma, Washington. Long before the Methodist church officially enabled women to become clergy, she was licensed to preach in 1920 and was ordained in 1926. Women were more valued in ecumenical work after Reverend Apel's employment as General

Secretary of the Council of Churches (a first).[104] The Church Council of Greater Seattle honors Reverend Apel by annually presenting an award in her name to two persons from the faith community who work to alleviate human suffering and social inequality.

The Seattle Council of Federated Church Women and The Seattle Council of Churches

From 1934 to 1935, Mrs. Robert Ralls served as President of the Seattle Council of Federated Church Women, as the group was then called.[105] On January 4, 1935, the first merger papers involving the Federated Church Women and the Seattle Council of Churches were drawn up. A resolution of cooperation was prepared by the joint committee and adopted by the Church Council's Board of Directors on February 4, 1937. The resolution stated: "There are now in Seattle, two inter-denominational church organizations working together: the Seattle Council of Churches and the Seattle Council of Federated Women."[106] This merger was viewed as a significant move by ecumenical organizations.

In 1933 to 1934 women served on many Seattle Council of Churches committees, including the Morals Committee, the Christian Education Committee, Social Service Committee, City Missions Committee, and the Inter-Church Committee. By 1945, The Seattle Council of Federated Women was called the Seattle Council of Church Women.[107] Mrs. A. K. Guy served as its President in 1946. By 1947, 150 churches belonged to the Seattle Council of Church Women, even though the women were still listed as a department of the Seattle Council of Churches.[108]

In 1950, the Seattle Council of Church Women held a World Community Service event at the First Methodist Church in Seattle. The annual theme was "Bundles of Bedding for the Homeless." Over 1,327 blankets were contributed at that event.[109]

51

Seattle Church Women United from 1960–2010

In 1962 the name of the movement was changed to United Church Women due to a recommendation from National CWU; however, in 1970 the group was renamed Church Women United and the name remains today.

Also, in 1962, Seattle Church Women United adopted its Constitution. Its preamble states: "Believing that in the providence of God, the time has come when it seems fitting more fully to manifest oneness in Jesus Christ as divine Lord and Savior."[110] The Christian Protestant women of Seattle adopted this Constitution and bylaws as a guide to promote the spirit of Christian fellowship, cooperation and service. The purpose of the organization was (1) "to unite Church women in their allegiance to their Lord and Savior Jesus Christ, through a program looking to their integration into the total life and work of the church and to the building of a world Christian community and (2) to provide an opportunity for Christian worship, fellowship, and service across denominational lines."[111]

In 1967 Mrs. Norma Clark served as President of SCWU. Under her leadership, the women were involved in many social action projects. For example: assistance to the Armed Services at the YMCA, the Women's Studio Club, Traveler's Aid, the Indian Center, the Veterans Hospital, the Foundation for International Understanding through Students, Seattle Public School's Volunteer Program, Seattle Opportunities Industrialization Center, and the Urban League's Operation Equality Project. "The women also continued to promote Church World Service's appeals: the Stamp Project, the Middle East Relief Fund, and the establishment of a Migrant Resettlement Project for migrant families."[112]

Mrs. Helen Bell's service as President of SCWU extended for three years from 1970 to 1972. In 1972, when faced with the

Boeing Company layoffs, the Neighbors in Need Food Banks were launched by the Church Council of Greater Seattle and SCWU. The women collected food from local churches and staffed the neighborhood distribution centers.[113] "It was truly an ecumenical experience as women of all faiths found themselves working side by side in serving their neighbors in need. This effort received national recognition and served as a model throughout the nation.

Mrs. Ann Williams Bush served as president of SCWU from 1975 to 1976. The Religious Committee for the Equal Rights Amendment (ERA) was formed in 1976 with SCWU as a key member. Members of SCWU wrote letters to Washington State legislators and Congress urging them to support ratification of the ERA. While SCWU and many others did all they could for the amendment to pass, it failed nationally.[114]

Three Seattle Women Who Transformed Lives

Mrs. Jeraldine Bright was the first African American to be elected president of the Seattle unit.[115] At this time, National CWU unveiled its new organizational plan; it gave each local unit the freedom to choose from among several action programs depending on the interests of its members. In accordance with the National CWU's major quadrennial priorities, Seattle's CWU chose the initiative Re-Assignment: Race.[116] Jeraldine

Bright, a member of the African Methodist Episcopal Church (AME), served as President of SCWU from 1977–1980. A woman of many gifts and talents, Mrs. Bright constantly struggled with the hypocrisy of Christian women who practiced racism and challenged them. Civil Rights and the issue of

racial justice and equality had been on CWU's agenda from its earliest days.

Motivated by her concern and passion for equality for all humankind, in 1980 she attended a national CWU planning meeting held at Green Lake, Wisconsin. As a national board member, she addressed the Executive Council and said "Church Women United must reaffirm common goals as Women of faith and select a quadrennial initiative on which we can all work together." She went on to say:

> We make beautiful speeches, embrace each other, sing when there is conflict and give our monetary gifts. I ask you, is this all there is to our faith? . . . Yet, we are called women of faith, but we will not and cannot journey toward wholeness and holiness in all of its richness and fullness until we work towards eliminating racism in all areas of our society. I ask you, how can we grow in faith and strengthen our ecumenical community, work for a just and caring society if there is hypocrisy within our own ranks? It will not happen as long as we have these internal conflicts. . .

> To be a reconciler during this time in our history means suffering. We need to take the cross from around our necks and off of the walls in our homes and put it in our hearts. I believe that the forgiving love of Christ breaks down barriers and sets us all free. Are you willing to put forth a greater effort for reconciliation, peace and justice? I ask you, Women of Faith, what is your answer?"[117]

Jeraldine Bright ended her presentation by acknowledging African American women as our sisters who have been subject

54

to racism and oppression more than other women in the United States.

She stood by her family during the storms of the ages and gave them love, affection, guidance, and prayer. Slavery taught the African American women to take the lead and heal the wounds of oppression which were deep and painful. She made the most of life when her men and sons were stolen from her. But her faith and hope in God strengthened the family and provided the incubator for the movement for liberation, pride, self-respect, and dignity.[118]

With the support of Dr. Thelma Adair, National President of CWU (1980–1984), a vote taken by the leaders resulted in the second initiative to eradicate racism within the ranks of CWU. This initiative was entitled Re-assignment Race. SCWU trained facilitators and forum leaders, as did other local units throughout the states and nation, to raise the consciousness of women to the pernicious evil of racism.

Additionally, SCWU conducted forums, workshops, and discussion groups during celebration events and ecumenical meetings. With a firm commitment to social justice, Mrs. Bright continued her endeavors to remove racism from within CWU and the Seattle area.

In 1978 "a Seattle Causeway on Urban Problems. . . brought national and foreign guests to Seattle to assist SCWU in learning more about the problems in urban communities."[119]

United Methodist church woman Janice Cate, from Bellevue, Washington, is a former National Board Member of Church Women United (CWU), Chair of the National Ecumenical Action Committee, President of Church Women United Washington and Northern Idaho from 1998–2000, and for years served as an officer with SCWU. Married to Dr.

55

William Cate, former President of the Church Council of Greater Seattle, Jan joined SCWU and brought with her a lifetime of ecumenical, interracial Christian activism, including her experience with the Women's International League for Peace and Freedom, and the Seattle Women Act for Peace organization.

Jan, a woman of courage and inspiration, called the women in Seattle to outrageous faithfulness. Working behind the scenes, she was rarely in the spotlight unless it was outside a courthouse after being arrested for civil disobedience, or leading and facilitating workshops and forums on direct action and social justice advocacy. In Seattle, she assisted in organizing the  Coalition Task Force on Women and Religion, and during the International Women's Decade. Jan, a game changer, was in the forefront of the struggle for change and women's rights.

For example, on December 18, 1972, the United Nations announced the observance of the International Women's Year in 1975, and at Plenary Session #2441 on December 15, 1975, it declared that 1976–1985 was the United Nation's Decade for Women. This declaration took place at the International Women's Year Conference in Mexico City.[120] The Declaration called for the "elimination of imperialism, colonialism, neocolonialism, foreign occupation, Zionism, alien domination, racism and apartheid," according to an editorial in the *Seattle Times*, July 6, 1975. SCWU and organizations in the religious community who participated in the decade's international conferences provided the attitudinal base of the ecumenical response to the decade's value theme: Peace, Equality and Economic Development.

Jan Cate founded the Peace Witness of Women in Black in the Greater Seattle Area and was one of the early supporters of the Church of Mary Magdalene, which will be discussed later in this chapter. Due to her influence, a section called "Women and Religion" was included in the monthly publication, *The Source,* an ecumenical newspaper published and distributed by the Church Council of Greater Seattle. The section was devoted to SCWU's calendar of events, international, national, and local peace and social justice articles, and the accomplishments of denominational women. In 1984, she wrote an article on The Feminization of Poverty and the consistency of the government to place the burden of funding militarism on the backs of women and children, particularly the poor.

Among her many awards, Jan Cate received an honorary Doctor of Humanities Degree from Seattle University. In June 1991, she also earned a Masters of Values and Ethics Degree from the Northwest Theological Union in Seattle. Her thesis was entitled: "The Response of Women in the Religious Community of Greater Seattle to the Stated Values of the International Women's Decade: Equality, Peace and Development, From the Grassroots Perspective of Peace."[121]

The Reverend Dr. Jean Kim, a Korean Presbyterian clergy woman was involved with the Korean Human Rights campaign. As a ten-year-old child, she walked from North Korea to South Korea with her brother to escape the Communists. She became part of the human rights struggle in South Korea but felt pressured to leave because many of the Korean Human Rights Community and religious leaders were being imprisoned. Many years later, she served for years as an outreach social worker on the streets of Seattle and became aware of homeless women's needs, such as a safe and nurturing spiritual home. She did not turn away from the needs of homeless women; instead she became a symbol of the Good Samaritan.

Reverend Kim gathered a multi-racial group of homeless women every week for a worship service and preached the Christian Gospel of acceptance, forgiveness, and hope. Many women, who attended the worship services, turned to God and accepted Jesus Christ as their Lord and Savior. In 1991, that small gathering of homeless women became the ecumenical Church of Mary Magdalene under the sponsorship of SCWU; Jean Kim was its first pastor.

Over twenty years later, the Church of Mary Magdalene is a racially and ethnically diverse Christian Community of homeless and formerly homeless women. The church has contributed to the empowerment of thousands of women and expanded its services. It now welcomes women to the church and provides meals every Saturday. Support for women who are in the hospital, incarcerated, or in need of pastoral care is also offered. The Reverend Dr. Jean Kim and SCWU's faith in the love and mercy of God has borne an abundance of fruit so that homeless and oppressed women can see the mercy of God.

Mary's Place was established in 1999 as an extension of The Church of Mary Magdalene's services to homeless women. Mary's Place provides emergency housing and aid to women and children in need of a day shelter, warm clothing, and food to eat. Today, Mary's Place is an independent social service agency.

Dr. Kim has served on the governor's Advisory Council on Homelessness in Washington State, the Interfaith Task Force on Homelessness, the National Presbyterian Network to End Homelessness, and the Korean American Coalition for the Homeless. Her manual on ending homelessness is a resource for congregations around the country. Among her many awards, she is the recipient of the Korean Medal of Honor.

A woman of vision and a heart filled with love, Jean Kim is in demand as an international speaker who continues to focus on impoverished women and children.

SCWU Expands Its Scope of Advocacy

In 1981 Cherie Babyack became President of CWU. During her term, the women monitored emergency rooms in response to reports of discrimination in gaining access to hospital emergency services. These reports included allegations of racial, economic, language, age, and gender barriers to accessing service in a timely manner. "The executive board of SCWU charged its members with the responsibility of investigating the accusations by spending at least one hour in the emergency waiting room in a hospital each day."[122]

When the United Nations declared the International Year of Disabled Persons in 1981, SCWU used care in selecting their event venues. The women made sure the buildings were accessible to accommodate those who were disabled.[123]

The people of El Salvador were also a major concern in the 1980s. SCWU cooperated with the Church Council of Greater Seattle in their study of conditions in Latin America. Accordingly, Seattle became one of the sanctuary cities providing refuge for people from El Salvador. The Church Council of Greater Seattle also played a major role in motivating religious groups in the area to oppose the United States' support of military governments in Central America[124] Moreover, in 1983, Church Women United endorsed "Public Sanctuary" as an ethical and legitimate Christian response to the persecution of refugees and as a means of alerting the American people to the human cost of the United States' policies related to Central America.[125]

Additionally, SCWU experienced the effectiveness of boycotts by bringing the attention of the community to the plight of the farm workers' struggle for better working conditions. The grape and lettuce boycotts were very effective in alleviating the inhumane conditions to which many migrant workers were subjected.[126]

While Mrs. Kay Wight served as SCWU President during the 1980s, military expenditures increased, while support for social programs declined. Yet, there was very little sympathy for people who depended on the government for help. President Reagan kept his campaign promise to increase defense spending and cut social welfare.[127] In response, SCWU wrote letters and publicly participated in demonstrations to show their opposition to increased militarism. In 1982 the following article concerning Nuclear War and the moral dilemma posed by the United States' military policies, was published in *The Source*:

> The United States is the world's largest exporter of arms, accounting for thirty-six percent of the total exports. Its military budget is now larger than the entire federal budget of twenty years ago. The issue of militarism was expounded on by the late Rev. Martin Luther King, Jr. over ten years ago. In his speech at the Riverside Church in New York City, entitled Beyond Vietnam, Dr. King had the perception to understand the inseparable link between the Civil Rights Movement and the struggle for global peace.
>
> Today, billions of dollars are going for military spending instead of programs which combat poverty, illiteracy, health services and unemployment. The largest and least discussed public health problem that would result from a relatively small nuclear explosion (1,455

megatons) would be how to dispose of the more than two million dead bodies resulting from senseless killings. The spiritual awareness and faith needed in the world today in order to combat these evils is being overshadowed by material goals which leave one's soul tragically empty. War is the direct result of greed and corruption. Peace, on the other hand, is an expression of God, and is manifested in justice, human rights, human dignity, reason, and love.[128]

Another advocacy effort by SCWU resulted from the World Health Organization's (WHO) adoption of an International Code of Marketing to stop the improper promotion of baby formulas. Companies who supplied milk for infants, such as Nestle and Bristol Meyers, continued to violate this code. They gave hospitals free supplies of formula on which the mothers became dependent. After leaving the hospitals, however, due to lack of money, the mothers used a diluted formula. This resulted in their babies having diarrhea and malnutrition, and some dying. To counteract this travesty, SCWU participated in the Infant Health Campaign by writing and boycotting Nestle and Bristol Meyers products.

Miss Imo Steele spearheaded this campaign and issued a call for women to write letters to Congress in support of full funding for breast-fed promotion programs by the WHO, UNICEF, and the United States Agency for International Development. Unfortunately, "Congress eliminated breastfeeding promotion from the agenda of U. S. aid and under pressure from the United States government, both UNICEF and the World Health Organization de-emphasized breastfeeding."[129]

In 1986, the National Board of CWU voted to implement a new imperative: to mobilize a movement that would address the pauperization and marginalization of women and children and to deal with the root causes of poverty and other related issues. Additionally, SCWU recognized that they could no longer minister to daily needs without also changing the circumstances that bring about poverty.

> A Washington State report on the Economic Status of Women (1986), compiled by Kim Nelson, pointed out that two out of three minimum wage workers are women, and one-third of women who are working full-time earn $7,000 or less a year. . . . If women were paid salaries equal to similarly qualified men, half of the poverty in this country would be eliminated. Compounding these factors is that four out of ten single mothers receive no support from the fathers of their children.[130]

Other factors leading to poverty included the following: deficiencies in affordable health and child care, lack of on-the-job training for jobs that pay a wage beyond poverty level, minimal available employment that pays comparable wages to that of men, the inability for women to save and invest due to the low wages they earn, and the lack of affordable pension plans for women who support their children.[131]

SCWU and Women in Black

In 1988, the Women in Black movement began as part of an international network of women who stand in silent vigil and call for peace, justice, and non-violent solutions to conflict. When Israeli women began lining busy streets and holding up signs protesting the Israeli occupation of Palestine, their persistence attracted media attention resulting in links with sympathetic groups all over the world. From 1991 to 1993 women in Belgrade protested against the wars throughout Yugoslavia, while New York City's Women in Black began a monthly vigil in solidarity with the Women in Black in Belgrade. By 2001, the movement continued to spread throughout the world.[132]

When the coveted Millennium Peace Prize for Women chose Women in Black as the recipient, Women in Black in Israel and Serbia represented the network because these two countries were on the forefront of insisting on dialogue and reconciliation, not war.[133]

Locally, Dr. Janice Cate, a former president of SCWU, inspired women to participate in Seattle's Women in Black, which had begun in 2001. At that time, Dr. Cate was an eighty-year-old great-grandmother and long-time peace activist. In 2003, with war in Iraq looming, Jan Cate decided it was time to bring the Women in Black message of peace to the east side of Lake Washington. She chose the city of Bellevue, a fast-growing upper-middle-class urban city, separated from Seattle by Lake Washington. The women's husbands often joined them at the vigil; their role was to hold signs or hand out leaflets. Members of Veterans for Peace also participated. Cate stated that she hoped by standing for peace and justice others will continue to join. . . . "I really do believe in this," she said, "it has to be done."[134]

Meanwhile, as SCWU continued its Women in Black vigils, the United Nations announced a January 15th deadline for Iraqi withdrawal from Kuwait. Encouraged, SCWU participated in an inter-faith candlelight peace procession on the eve of the deadline. The route began at St. Mark's Cathedral (Episcopal) and ended at St. James Cathedral (Roman Catholic) with prayers by Christian, Jewish, Muslim, and SCWU leaders. It was the largest national ecumenical public witness for peace and anti-United States military involvement.[135]

63

The Church of Mary Magdalene

In 1991, Presbyterian clergywoman Jean Kim, an officer with SCWU, founded the Church of Mary Magdalene. A decade later, Reverend Patricia Simpson, a United Methodist clergywoman and former member of SCWU, pastored the Church of Mary Magdalene for more than eight years. She provided pastoral care and the leadership to expand its services. In 1999, the women added the weekday program entitled Mary's Place to minister to women and children in need of a place to go during the day.

Material assistance was also a part of the ministry from the start. The Church of Mary Magdalene provided nourishing food and helped with housing and emergency aid. Gifts, such as new lingerie added a special touch affirming the women's dignity. The ministry was able to continue helping the homeless, in the name of Jesus Christ, because of support from various denominations.

Reverend Linda Smith was called to pastor in 2009. In 2011 the board of directors made the decision to form two separate ministries: the Church of Mary Magdalene and Mary's Place. Both programs empowered women and children to reclaim their lives. Each Saturday, Reverend Smith preached to the ecumenical gathering of homeless and formerly homeless women and children. Congregational singing and Bible study were highlighted during the day. Special programs, arts and crafts, and other creative and practical opportunities were also provided. Today, the two-in-one ministry is flourishing. In 2014, for a short while, Reverend Kelle Brown became pastor at the Church of Mary Magdalene, carrying on the important role of caring for women. She also stood in silent vigil with Women in Black to protest the unjustifiable shootings of young African American males.

Thanks to SCWU and Reverend Jean Kim's vision, and the pastoral care of Reverends Kim, Simpson, Smith, and Brown, countless homeless women and children have their physical, social, and spiritual needs met.

SCWU and the World Day of Prayer

CWU celebrations were especially popular throughout the Greater Seattle area, and Christian women looked forward to SCWU's celebrations with great anticipation. For example, each year SCWU held their World Day of Prayer (WDP) celebration in at least ten Seattle churches. The Bible study, prayer, and re-dedication service included women from every class, race, and ethnic group. The women who wrote the study and service program for the WDP celebration incorporated the needs of the women and children living in the countries they represented.[136]

The courageous Christian women, who served as officers and members of SCWU were committed to the mission and goals of the movement. Each president mentioned in this chapter, left an indelible legacy in the hearts and minds of those they empowered. Through their visible witness of love, compassion, social justice, and peace, they inspired women from all walks of life. Whether it was petitioning the government to ratify the Equal Rights Amendment, developing a program to combat racism, demonstrating against militarism, or being involved with the Infant Health Campaign, everything they accomplished was done in the name of our Lord and Savior Jesus Christ. It is no wonder the Seattle faith and wider community are grateful for the programs created by the visions and faith of Seattle's CWU.

Seattle's Current Ecumenical Engagement

Seattle is blessed to have two organized ecumenical resources able to engage others in purposeful dialogue. The first is Seattle University's School of Theology and Ministry (STM), which educates and informs faith leaders from some 13 denominations with whom they partner. In this rich ecumenical environment the men and women enrolled as students at STM are being prepared to serve the church and the world by offering effective and mature leadership in their respective ministries. The constant ecumenical exchange and the diverse theological perspectives in their classes provide students with an unparalleled experience. When they leave seminary, graduates step into their ministry prepared to meet the realities of religious diversity.

The second resource, the Church Council of Greater Seattle, is a visible symbol of cooperation among fifteen Christian denominations that carry forward the vision and belief that all humanity and all creation belong to God and are loved by God. Through the Church Council structure, Christian congregations, judicatories, organizations, and individuals respond to the Holy Spirit in our midst, through a deepening of mutual accompaniment in anticipation of God's shalom. Today, most of the programming is driven by current commitments in the areas of social justice and social services. Each year the Council convenes the ecumenical Assembly to celebrate our unity and collaboration, to provide direct engagement with members and constituencies, to solicit strategic feedback, and gain new insights for planning and discernment of the Board's mission.

The Church Council functions as a unit in the ecumenical movement and has sustained relationships with the National Council of Churches and the World Council of Churches. Up until Seattle's CWU unit closed, the Church Council of Greater Seattle provided SCWU leaders with a permanent seat on the board of directors and the status of equal partner.

CHAPTER SIX

THEOLOGICAL PERSPECTIVES

Christian women involved in SCWU accepted the charge to pursue Christian unity among women through social justice advocacy and Liberation Theology. The women believed that each CWU generation should respond to those who suffer (particularly women and children) from hunger, poverty, racism, and other systemic forms of oppression. They accomplished this by studying the issue, reading, reflecting on the scriptures through the eyes of those suffering, and acting in faith for justice on their behalf.

The text that follows explores the social gospel and the application of Liberation Theology through the theological perspectives of four people of faith, whose ideals reflect the values of CWU: *Walter Rauschenbusch's* development and application of the social gospel in response to a social crisis during the late nineteenth century; *Archbishop Oscar Romero's* response to the suffering poor in El Salvador; *Dr. Mossie Allman Wyker*, ordained minister and former national Church Women United president, who worked to liberate women from patriarchal oppression; and *The Reverend Dr. Martin Luther King, Jr.,* a civil rights leader who responded non-violently to individual and institutional racism in America. Each liberator engaged in social justice work and used a form of Liberation Theology as a framework for their social justice advocacy.

The ideals of these four remarkable theologians are made manifest in two of CWU's goals: "(1) to work for a just, peaceful, and caring society, (2) and to use the resources God has entrusted in us: our intelligence, time, energy, and our money responsibly and creatively, as we carry out the mission of Christ."[137]

Liberation theology involves the liberation of the oppressed as directly derived through their faith experience. It develops within an individual and group through three fundamental moments: seeing, judging, and acting. Within this context, there are two mediations: the socio-analytic mediation, which contemplates the world of the oppressed; and the hermeneutic mediation, which contemplates and reflects on the word of God to see what the divine language reveals. At this point, the scriptures are confronted through the eyes of the poor, thereby creating a new reading of the Bible, the hermeneutics of liberation. This process activates the transforming energy of the biblical text to action.[138]

The conclusion of this chapter synthesizes themes and values discovered in the content. These themes are convictions that unite these four theologians with the values of CWU, because all four committed themselves to implementing the social principles of Jesus Christ.

Theologian Walter Rauschenbusch (1861–1918)

"Christianity in its nature is revolutionary."

Walter Rauschenbusch

Walter Rauschenbusch, often called the prophet of social Christianity, was born in New York City. After finishing his theological education, he became the pastor of a small German Baptist Church in New York City situated on the edge of Hell's Kitchen.[139] As its name suggests, this area was one of extreme poverty because of the hostility toward unskilled German immigrants. More established European-Americans believed the immigrants threatened the traditional American culture, institutions, and the social order. In the space of a single generation, a few hundred corporate leaders gained tremendous wealth and economic power, although many of their industries were unhealthy or even dangerous for the immigrants— especially for women and children. Rauschenbusch claimed that this crisis results from conflict between the well-being of the masses of the population and the vested interest of the powerful. He further contended that American Capitalism had produced a fundamentally unjust social and economic system. Thus, he wanted to create a new society in which the major structures would support a more equitable distribution of resources and wealth.[140]

Capitalism is an economic system based on economic freedom for the individual. Adam Smith (1723–1809), a Scottish philosopher and economist, was the first to describe capitalism in his book the *Wealth of Nations* published in 1776. "From Smith's writings came the idea of Laissez-faire economics, a French term which means to 'let alone.'"[141] This aspect of capitalism, limits the government's role to insure free competition and profit in the market place.

Rauschenbusch and the social gospel movement were committed to correcting the pervasive social injustices arising from the Laissez-faire philosophy. He became the founder and leading spokesperson for the movement arguing that serving Christ meant working for the equality and happiness of all persons. "Other theologians also agreed that the teachings of Christ did not support a strictly capitalistic economy of production and profit. Instead, social religion grounded in the teachings and example of Christ, not materialism, was the key to well being and success."[142]

From that mindset Rauschenbusch began his social justice advocacy by writing and publishing books. In his manuscript *Christianity Revolutionary* (1891), Rauschenbusch believed that the kingdom of God had been central to the ministry of Jesus and the early mission of the church. This social ideology grew gradually and integrated social idealism with spiritual reality.[143]

Between 1907 and 1917, the themes of crisis and opportunity were reflected throughout the books Rauschenbusch published. He wrote *Christianity and the Social Crisis* in 1907; it gained prominence and recognition among liberal Christian Protestants.[144] His main thesis is that Christianity at the beginning of the twentieth century confronted a social crisis that offered the followers of Jesus Christ, who were enlightened by the Holy Spirit, an unparalleled opportunity to work for a social order that would fit more harmoniously with the demands of the Kingdom of God.[145] Rauschenbusch analyzed the ethical and social message of the Old Testament Prophets and Jesus' message as they applied to the social conditions and suffering poor. *Christianity and the Social Crisis* was skillfully fashioned and perfectly timed.

> Rauschenbusch's book became the catalyst for the Social Gospel Movement, and went through thirteen printings in five years, sold 50,000 copies, and set a new standard for political theology. He more than any other theologian made American Christians aware of the abuses and injustices arising out of the Industrial Revolution.[147]

His theological themes on the social gospel evolved from his perspective on a universal ideology regarding the nature of sin. He wrote that "sin cannot be grasped without viewing the human condition and that traditional theology's focus on the biological transmission of evil through Adam and Eve neglected to include the power of the social transmission of evil through social, political and economic systems."[147]

Social salvation was another theological theme that Rauschenbusch developed. He believed that individual salvation and the salvation of a society were intertwined. Indeed, according to Rauschenbusch, there are two aspects of one gospel: (1) the gospel in its spiritual dimension, and (2) the gospel in its social dimension. Thus, he believed that genuine salvation turns men and women from self to God and humanity; in this approach, salvation is the voluntary socializing of the soul."[148] Rauschenbusch's understanding of Christ's mission, purpose, and death is to be understood through the Kingdom of God, where God invites all humans to become brothers and sisters in a universal fellowship of love and righteousness. It is a dynamic power in history, redeeming both humankind and the social structures that shape life.[149]

Walter Rauschenbusch's books had a huge impact at liberal seminaries and the social gospel ecumenical movement in the United States that prevailed for years. "His was an enduring perspective that paved the way for Modern Ecumenism, such as Social Christianity, and the ecumenical and social justice ministries that remain the heart of American Christianity."[150]

Today, a Rauschenbusch Center is active in Seattle, and although established by the Reverend David Bloom and the congregation of the University Baptist Church, it is now a program of the Church Council of Greater Seattle. The Center functions as an ecumenical organization with outreach to congregations and individuals of various religious traditions and is committed to fostering theological education and theological reflection on issues and problems facing society.

Archbishop Oscar Romero (1917–1980)

"A church that suffers no persecution but enjoys the privileges and support of the things of the earth—beware!—is not the true church of Jesus Christ. A preaching that does not point out sin is not the preaching of the gospel."

Oscar Romero

Poverty in Latin America gave rise to Liberation Theology. According to the proponents of that theology, experiencing God in Latin America meant hearing the voice of God in the cries of the poor, the oppressed, and the marginalized millions. Too, it is hearing the word of God through the prophets and the life and ministry of Jesus Christ. It is also realizing that the institutional violence and domination in Latin America is backed by the wealthy and the military. Herein lies the paradox:

> The more we are conscious of the oppressive forces and structures of society, the more we become able to understand the word of God concealed by these forces. And, the more we understand the liberating word of God in human history, the more we are confronted with inhuman and unjust structures in our society."[151]

What is a theology of liberation? It is a process grounded in Christian love which requires a good understanding of social and economic systems, institutions, and other factors that produce injustices and violence. Mediation is a means adopted by its theology to achieve its goal to integrate the parts that constitute liberation according to theologians. This includes seeing the socio/political environment through the eyes of the poor, judging in light of the scriptures (the hermeneutics of liberation) and acting both pastorally or practically in light of this information.

72

Through evangelical conversion, the hope that prevails is that the oppressors will become sisters and brothers to the poor.[152]

The story of the faith experience of the poor of El Salvador helps one articulate the theological context of Latin-American Liberation Theology. The aristocracy and military controlled the indigenous Indian people. Rooted in the Roman Catholic faith tradition, the Salvadorans were subjected to institutionalized violence that caused poverty, oppression, and even death. Church leaders were corrupt and controlled by the rich and the military. The basis for these injustices included classism, the need for land reform, and greed. Sadly, the United States was involved with supplying arms to El Salvador's oppressive government.[153] Moreover, several priests had been murdered for attempting to offer communion and Mass for the poor. Due to this horrendous situation, Father Oscar Romero was appointed by the Salvadoran Bishop's Conference to the position of Archbishop to El Salvador.[154]

Archbishop Romero's faith position was that the mission of the church is to identify with the poor and oppressed. In doing so, the church finds its own salvation. Therefore, the poor served as the locus to illustrate and explain the social principles of Jesus. Archbishop Romero believed that a church in solidarity with the poor can denounce poverty as an evil. "The church," he said, "would betray its own love for God and its fidelity to the gospel if it stopped being a defender of the rights of the poor."

Archbishop Romero was transformed, by the Scriptures, to respond as Christ. He knew it was the poor and oppressed who were the lost, battered, and hungry souls in Jesus' parable of the Good Samaritan (Luke 10:33). He refused to accept the present situation of the poor and felt great indignation in the presence of injustice and violence. He interpreted his social reality from the point of view of the faith experience lived by the poor. He

73

reflected on this reality in the interest of the victims and holy Scriptures and acted in solidarity with them.

Jesus said, "Greater love hath no man than this, that a man lay down his life for his friends" (John 15:13). Although he was forbidden by the military and government of El Salvador to offer Mass for the poor people of El Salvador, Archbishop Romero was committed to allowing the blessings of God to flow freely to indigenous Salvadoran Christians. He loved his brothers and sisters so much that he died for them; he was shot in the heart while offering Mass.

As a martyr, Archbishop Romero ignited a world-wide response. His act inspired hundreds of Americans who provided sanctuaries for the people who fled El Salvador. CWU's public statements and resolutions were sent to the United States government to protest the role of the United States in El Salvador. These actions eventually brought about a semblance of peace to the Salvadoran people. Archbishop Romero exemplified CWU's values lived out through Liberation Theology. His story continues to remind people about the liberating power of a compassionate Savior.

Dr. Mossie Allman Wyker (1901–1988)

"Women are essential in the scheme of things because they are beloved daughters of the heavenly king."

Mossie Allman Wyker

A feminist theology of liberation is not just a theoretical world view or perspective. Rather, it is a women's liberation movement for societal and ecclesiastical change in any situation where women suffer the injustices of oppression in patriarchal structures. It remains first and foremost a critical theology of liberation.

A good example of Christ as liberator is the story of Jesus' encounter with Mary and Martha in Luke 10:38–41. During Jesus' time, women could not attend the synagogue to learn unless their husbands were rabbis. For a rabbi to come into a woman's home and teach her was forbidden and counter-cultural. Nevertheless, Jesus risked the possibility of public scandal to teach Mary (Luke10). As Mary listened and sat at Jesus' feet, he challenged the patriarchal framework of the Jewish culture. Jesus went beyond rules, limitations, social norms, and other cultural and societal traditions to share with Mary the love and transforming word of God.

Reverend Mossie Allman Wyker, an ordained minister, worked to liberate women from patriarchal oppression, in and out of the church. After being successful as the President of UCW in Ohio, she played an important role in the early work of two ecumenical organizations whose origins were intertwined: United Church Women and the National Council of Christian Churches. At the Assembly in Cincinnati, Ohio, Reverend Wyker's name was placed in nomination as the first chairperson of the General Department of United Church Women at the Constituting Convention of the National Council of Christian Churches.

Further, as President of United Church Women, Reverend Wyker focused particularly on improving race relations. "She realized that African American women did not enjoy the same access to power and influence as their white sisters. From 1956 to 1960, she also served UCW as Minister at Large focusing on supporting and encouraging local pastors who were trying to deal faithfully with racial tensions gripping the country."[155] As one of the important women speakers of her time on behalf of women, she provided hope for all church women.

Mossie Wyker's early ecumenical work led her to write about the role of women in the church in her book, *Church Women in the Scheme of Things*. Her focus was based on her experience with CWU. She wrote that "women are essential in the scheme of things because they are beloved daughters of the heavenly king."[156] In her book, she does not plead for equal rights but for the equal opportunity for women to use their God-given talents for the glory of God. She believed that the strength of church women, who were united, provided alternative solutions to important social issues.[157]

In particular, she urged women not to be second-class citizens in their churches and to use their talents as they saw fit. She was critical of the Apostle Paul and his statements that women should keep silent in the church. Wyker wrote: "Paul's ministry would have been greatly weakened were it not for Lydia, Priscilla, Lois, Dorcas, and Phoebe."[158] She admonished the women that they would not be satisfied until they attained their utmost potential and followed where God was leading them.

The ordination of women was important to Reverend Wyker. She did not agree that women should oppose the ordination of their sisters who want to preach the gospel and serve the church with their spiritual gifts. Through her speaking engagements and her writings, Reverend Wyker motivated, challenged, and called women forth to live their vocation. For example, Reverend Wyker wrote about the courage of Methodist Antoinette Brown Blackwell (1825–1921), American minister and social reformer, whose foremost desire was to preach the Gospel of Jesus Christ. "Overcoming numerous obstacles, she eventually became the first American woman to be ordained as a pastor."[159]

To honor Reverend Mossie Wyker's life of service, Transylvania College awarded her a Doctor of Divinity degree. She died on July 2, 1988, but through her legacy of courage and commitment to all women, she inspired them to press on with faith in God.[165]

Today, women clergy have made impressive progress. No one knows the exact count, but a survey estimates that approximately 10 percent of American congregations have a female as their senior or sole ordained leader. The Faith Communities Today's 2010 national survey of a fully representative, multi-faith sample of 11,000 American congregations found that 12 percent of all congregations in the United States had a female as their sole ordained leader. For old-line Protestant congregations this jumps to 24 percent and for Evangelical congregational it drops to 9 percent.

From an historic view, a Duke University study revealed that eleven percent of main-line Protestant churches are led by women. For example, 18.5 percent of all United Methodist clergy are women and 36 percent of students in degree programs at seminaries are women. Further, a study undertaken in the mid-1990s by Barbara Brown Zikmund, Adair Lummis, and Patricia Change discovered that the more theologically liberal groups such as the Unitarian Universalist Association and the United Church of Christ lead in the percent of their clergy who are female with thirty and twenty-five, respectively. On the other hand, the most theologically conservative groups, such as the Southern Baptist Convention, the Free Methodist Church and the Assemblies of God all have less than 10 percent of their pastors being female.

A special historical note is that for the first time in the history of the eighty-three year old interdenominational mainline Protestant Riverside Church in Manhattan, New York, a female was elected Senior Minister. The Reverend Dr. Amy Butler follows renowned social justice Senior Ministers such as the Reverend Dr. Sloan Coffin, Jr., and the Reverend Dr. James Alexander Forbes, who is presently Minister Emeritus. It is hoped that the day will come when women will not be judged on the basis of their gender but for who they are in Christ.

Reverend Dr. Martin Luther King, Jr. (1929–1968)

"I believe that unarmed truth and unconditional love will have the final word in reality. That is why right temporarily defeated, is stronger than evil triumphant. Our lives begin to end the day we become silent about things that matter."

Reverend Dr. Martin Luther King, Jr.

The historical, social, and political environment in which the Reverend Dr. Martin Luther King, Jr., developed his ministry and formed his theology, contained daily reminders of social and institutional racism. African Americans were denied the civil rights granted by the U.S. Constitution to all citizens. In response to this crisis, Dr. King, an African American Baptist preacher, interpreted Jesus' life and ministry within a social context and confronted injustice. In doing so, he became an instrument of social transformation amidst ideological conflicts between the white and black races in America.[160]

During the civil rights movement in the 1960s, Dr. King addressed the massive problems in race relations. He opposed individual bigotry and the systematic institutionalization of racism through laws and social systems. He also believed that racial injustices in America were rooted in an ideological racism that had been used as an excuse for slavery. When slave holders rationalized slavery and clothed it in garments of righteousness, they developed the theory of white supremacy."[161]

Although African Americans were granted equal rights and protection under the 14th Amendment (1868) to the Constitution and given the right to vote by passage of the 15th Amendment (1870), in practice they were still denied those rights. Yet, African Americans still paid taxes and fought in wars (albeit in segregated units) to protect the very system that oppressed them. Treated like second-class citizens, African Americans could not attend the best schools, parks, or restaurants, and were made to sit in the back of buses and ride in segregated railroad cars.[162]

The social revolution that emerged from this milieu was designed to bring a radical change in the very structure of national life. Justice, King felt, required equal opportunity in the social order for African Americans who had been exploited by society; this was his mission. Reflecting on the word of God through the eyes of African Americans who suffered all kinds of degradation, Dr. King proceeded to apply the social gospel as the basis of his appeal for social reform. Jesus Christ became the example King followed. He said:

> Where do we find God? In a test tube? No, where else except in Jesus Christ! By knowing him we know God. Christ is not only Godlike but God is Christ like. Christ is the word made flesh. He is the language of eternity translated in the words of time. If we are to know what God is like and understand his purpose for humankind, we must turn to Christ. And by committing ourselves absolutely to Christ and his way, we will participate in that marvelous act of faith that will bring us to the true knowledge of God.[163]

Just as Jesus indicted the Romans and the Jews, who were responsible for oppressing the people during that time, King followed Jesus' example and called for action leading to social reform that would bring justice to those who were deprived.

Dr. King knew that his call for change also meant he had to exemplify the love of God to his enemies. He preached the inclusive love of Christ and the gift of salvation. For example, Jesus was a friend to the friendless. He made friends with tax collectors and called one of them to be his disciple (Mt. 10:13). He also called two fishermen, Peter, and his brother Andrew, to become fishers of men (Mk. 4:19).

To the women, Jesus brought justice, liberty, mercy, and forgiveness. He ministered to the woman who was being stoned when caught in the act of adultery (Jn.8:1–9) and to the Samaritan woman, considered an outcast by society, he offered living water (Jn.4:10). To the poor and oppressed, Jesus gave assurance of God's love and mercy through his Sermon on the Mount where he said, "Blessed are the poor in Spirit for theirs is the Kingdom of heaven" (Matt. 5:3). Clearly, King's understanding of the teachings and ministry of Jesus Christ profoundly influenced his life as he sought to bring about a revolution of social and spiritual values through non-violence.

Jesus told Peter to "put up his sword, for those that live by the sword shall die by the sword" (Jn.18:10–11). Jesus knew humility and declared to his disciples the true nature of spiritual greatness. Jesus called the twelve and said to them, "If any man desires to be first, the same shall be last of all and servant of all" (Mk. 9:35). Dr. King turned down the call to pastor an influential affluent Baptist church in Atlanta, Georgia. Instead, he chose to serve those who were marginalized and denied the right to life, liberty and the pursuit of happiness.

"In the morning, rising up a great while before day, he went out and departed into a solitary place and prayed" (Mk 1:35). Dr. King also knew the power of prayer. He and his followers prayed before every march or demonstration. Jesus spoke of forgiveness and when he was asked how many times a person should forgive, he answered "seventy times seven" (Matt.

18:22). King believed in this precept and turned the other cheek, as an act of forgiveness, when he was confronted by segregationists with whips and vicious police dogs.

Dr. King was also concerned about the Church. He believed that the Church had an opportunity and duty to lift up its voice and denounce the immorality of racism and segregation. He wanted church leaders to affirm that every human life is a reflection of divinity and every act of injustice mars and defaces the image of God in man.[164] King's widow, Coretta Scott King, noted that King "challenged the church with this question: If the church is called to serve humanity in God's name, what kind of examples are church leaders giving when they fail to stand up for justice?"[165] As another succinctly remarked "Dr. King wanted the church to confess its racism and…truancy to its true Christian heritage."[166]

Like Rauschenbusch, King believed that the social gospel is as important as the gospel of personal salvation. He stated: "Any religion that professes to be concerned about the souls of men and ignores social and economic conditions that cripple the soul is a dead religion, only waiting to be buried."[167]

Dr. Martin Luther King, Jr., left a legacy of hope and love across the history of this nation when he rose to challenge discrimination and inequality towards Afro-Americans and all oppressed people.

Church Women United, theologian Reverend Walter Rauschenbusch, Archbishop Oscar Romero, Dr. Mossie Wyker, and The Reverend Dr. Martin Luther King, Jr., all practiced a form of Liberation Theology that was an outgrowth of the social gospel. All four liberationists sought to implement Liberation Theology by embracing a commitment to the poor, marginalized, and disenfranchised.

Reverend Rauschenbusch read the scriptures and concluded that traditional theology had diverted the minds of the religious corporate and factory owners to profitability; this diversion powered the social transmission of evil. He also interpreted the Christian message in terms of social redemption, because he believed the gospel in its social dimension had been neglected.

Archbishop Romero put into practice the hermeneutics of liberation, which had been developed by many of the Latin-American Catholic liberation theologians. Reading the scriptures through the eyes of poor Salvadorans, who were victims of injustice and oppression, Archbishop Romero came to know their social reality and their faith experience. He stood in solidarity with the suffering Salvadorans and acted on their behalf. When he gave his life, Archbishop Romero ignited a worldwide response which, in turn, advanced the cause of liberation throughout Latin America.

Dr. Mossie Wyker witnessed the oppression that many of her sisters experienced. She reflected on the word of God in her speeches and writings. She advocated and exhorted women to have the courage to use their God-given talents in the way God would have them. She believed church women have a significant role to play in the destiny of humankind, as evidenced by her many years of service to CWU. God placed within her the gift of encouragement as she wrote to inspire women to acknowledge that God placed within them the longing to help make a better world.

The Reverend Dr. Martin Luther King, Jr. responded to the suffering of African Americans by interpreting Jesus' life and ministry within a social context. Reverend King interpreted the Gospel to mean that all forms of racism, whether individual, collective, or systemic must be named sin and their theological justification named heresy. The redemptive vision of Dr. King still lives on in the hearts of those who believe in true democracy and equality for all.

Thus, all four liberationists witnessed, in their own way, to the love of Christ for all humankind. Themes and values developed from their beliefs clearly delineate their commonalities, which are also reflected in the mission, values, goals, and praxis of Church Women United.

Like CWU, each theologian was led by the Holy Spirit to carry out the mission of Christ and fashion the Kingdom of God "on earth as it is in heaven." Like CWU, each theologian stood against the powers of evil and advocated for equality, justice, faith, and transformation.

Common Themes and Values
of the Four Theologians

THEMES	VALUES
Liberation Theology	*Liberty*
Social Gospel	Justice, love, compassion, and mercy
Social Redemption	Morality, forgiveness, brother and sister-hood
Social Salvation	Inclusiveness, transformation
Kingdom of God	Reign of God on Earth, love, faith, and obedience to God's word
Equal Rights	Justice/righteousness, equality
Hermeneutic of Liberation	Scriptural reflection through the eyes of the oppressed
Civil Rights	Protection, freedom, equality
Praxis	Courage, action, advocacy Christian, faith, belief, love

CHAPTER SEVEN

QUESTIONS POSED ABOUT SCWU'S CLOSURE AND THE RESPONSES

The Seattle faith community and the broader community sought answers to what led to and caused the SCWU unit to close; therefore, this book was undertaken to create an accurate holistic account of the factors and events surrounding SCWU's closure.

Through study and interviews with SCWU former officers and participants, as well as others who knew its work, helpful information emerged. Using open-ended questions, such as those noted below, helped determine the factors that people believed contributed to SCWU's closure.

- What is one story you would like to share about the positive impact SCWU made?
- What is the strength and legacy of SCWU?
- Why did SCWU decide to close and what protocols were followed?
- How was the decision to close the unit made?
- What could have been done to prevent SCWU from closing?

These questions allowed additional questions, answers, and recollections to emerge. Particular attention was given to identifying consistent trends among the responses. Those interviewed could answer questions in a way that was most comfortable for them.

Since the author relied on information gathered in consultation with former SCWU officers and members, responses could not be projected to a large population of CWU units.

In addition to querying SCWU's former officers or members, denominational diversity was also considered important for gathering a cross-section of ecumenical perspectives. Christian women from ages sixty-five to ninety, and with a racial make-up that included Asian, African American, Caucasian, and Latino were invited to provide feedback. Most were lay-women in their churches; however, two were ordained ministers. The women had varying levels of education, most were retired, and all were committed to social justice. In all, fourteen women participated in roundtables and interviews.

The profoundly deep and moving responses shared by those queried cannot be adequately captured by extensive statistical analysis. However, careful examination of their responses to questions about SCWU revealed key words, statements, and main points shared by the responders. While questions generated a lengthy list of remarks, in each person's exact words, the clustered feedback indicated that some ideas were not mutually exclusive and some might overlap. Idea clusters were organized into the following categorical headings: historical, sociological, cultural, and theological. Some common patterns of particular interest surfaced, and these are noted in the responses listed here.

Questions and Aggregated Participant Responses

Question One: What is one story you would like to share about the positive impact SCWU made?

Historical Lens: SCWU women were empowered to exercise the gifts God had given them in both ministry and administrative responsibilities. There were also multiple experiences of intergenerational benefits due to SCWU's inclusiveness. Younger women learned from the older women and brought new insights and enthusiasm. Each shared the joy of praising the Lord and fellowshipping with one another during the celebrations. Christian women of all races and classes also embraced the opportunity to alleviate suffering through mission, peace, and social justice advocacy.

Sociological Lens: Great value was seen in giving aid to impoverished women and children either by supporting or participating in SCWU-sponsored programs such as Dress for Success and The Church of Mary Magdalene.

Theological Lens: In the faith-based Christian fellowship dimension, the World Day of Prayer was significant because of the ecumenical involvement, scripturally based non-denominational Bible studies, and corporate prayer.

Question Two: What was SCWU's strength and legacy?

Historical Lens: SCWU offered women opportunities for growth and leadership in a male-dominated society. Unique as a movement, Christian women were invited to join regardless of race, denominational affiliation, and economic status.

Sociological Lens: SCWU women were strong, courageous role models who had compassion for those in need. Christian women, who often felt isolated, were inspired and drawn to SCWU through neighborhood relationships when planning Celebrations. The women also felt a sense of belonging and sisterhood. They became empowered, grew more knowledgeable about social justice issues, and were able to freely express their ideals.

Cultural Lens: SCWU promoted a culture of unity and love in spite of its diverse constituency of races, ethnicities, social classes, and denominations. This gave all women, who had a passion for social justice, an opportunity to meet and work with other like-minded women who desired to channel their love into action.

Theological Lens: SCWU's legacy of spirituality, prayer, bible study, and action was a visible witness of God's love for humanity. The women were gratified to advocate for those in need as they followed the example of Jesus Christ.

Question Three: Why did SCWU decide to close and what protocols were followed?

Historical Lens: Three responses indicated that the president resigned and the vice-president refused to function. All fourteen responders stated that they were unaware of national CWU's protocol to close a unit.

Sociological Lens: Many answers disclosed that the unit focused on a single issue which caused them to be less visible and viable in the faith and broader communities. Moreover, the interview participants felt SCWU's aging membership had no outreach plan to recruit younger women. According to those queried, the average age of an SCWU member was between seventy and eighty-five. Many of the women had health issues and were weary. Seven women stated that societal changes, such as the gentrification of Seattle may also have had an impact.

Cultural Lens: The emergence of other social justice organizations may have captured the hearts of the younger women, and some former members also felt that SCWU did not do enough to pass the mantle to younger Christian women. Respondents remarked that meetings were not always welcoming to others, and some women stated that they were not consistently informed about when and where the meetings were being held. Some felt that the second generation of Baby Boomers were self-centered and materialistic and therefore lacked interest in long-term commitments to a movement. Many felt that SCWU officers had their own agenda and were not interested in recruiting others.

Theological Lens: Participants felt that declining denominational support and involvement from pastors and churches may have been because SCWU no longer held their meetings in churches and did not emphasize the theological aspects of CWU enough.

Question Four: How was the decision to close made?

Historical Lens: Most of the women, when asked, stated that they did not know how or who made the decision to close SCWU; however, one person said the decision to close was made by the executive officers. Historically, national CWU, regional, and state leaders were informed prior to a unit closing, but this did not occur in the closure of SCWU.

Sociological Lens: The participants affirmed that women just stopped attending. They believed women lost interest and seemed to call it quits without an explanation.

Cultural Lens: SCWU's closure left a void in the community and diminished its ability to positively impact Seattle's culture.

Theological Lens: The former members believed that when SCWU closed, it denied the people of Seattle a tremendous Christian witness to faith in Jesus Christ and the social justice advocacy that leads to transformed lives.

Question Five: What could have been done, if anything, to save SCWU?

Historical Lens: The women queried felt that SCWU should have taken the initiative to reconnect with the history of SCWU and pass it on to younger women.

Sociological Lens: Some participants believed that SCWU should have remained focused on the mission and goals of national CWU and stayed better connected to the regional and state units.

Cultural Lens: The women questioned believed that if SCWU had told the story of the CWU movement more often throughout the faith community, it would have drawn in women

89

who had a passion for social justice and this would have increased SCWU membership.

Theological Lens: Had SCWU provided a standard meeting time and church venue, more denominational women and pastors would have remained informed and involved. All the responders agreed that SCWU should have prayed for more faith and strength to carry on (See Appendix D).

CHAPTER EIGHT

SUMMARY OF FINDINGS

Some in the Seattle faith community need answers regarding why SCWU disappeared, since no formal explanation exists as to why, how, and what caused the unit to close. The Seattle Unit of Church Women United was a powerful presence and, in many ways, its witness continues. Finding answers about the closure, however, is to no purpose if nothing is learned, no action is taken, and no change occurs. SCWU's rich tradition is such that even though closed, it will produce good fruit—if in no other way than to teach lessons to others who rise up to advocate for justice and equality.

Sending a summary of lessons learned—conclusions and recommendations, if you will—to the CWU national president, executive officers, Washington State officers, and the Northwest regional coordinator can help strengthen the movement as a whole. The information gleaned can serve as a cautionary signal.

From the results of interview questions noted in the previous chapter some conclusions can be offered.

Church Women United is largely shaped by historical, sociological, cultural, and theological dynamics. Challenges occur when analyzing events because of CWU's interconnected framework, (i.e., the national, regional, state, and local units of the CWU movement have horizontally linked interrelated parts, as opposed to having a vertical organizational structure). Still, CWU gave Christian Women an opportunity for discipleship and service to others locally, nationally, and internationally.

The formal organization of this ecumenical movement was a result of Christian Women's groups fulfilling their mission in local communities throughout the U.S. and around the world. Concerns and prayers for impoverished women and children in

Asia and Africa led to various local and state church women federations, and these ultimately led to a national movement with a national Constitution and By-laws that governed state and local units. The movement was an avenue for Christian women to work together in the vineyard as instruments of Christ's reconciling love and redemption to the least, the lost, and the left out.

As the Spirit of God moved, it touched and convicted the hearts of the women to unite and work for unity, justice, and peace; that was their mission. The women studied, prayed, celebrated, and went forth, not limiting their concerns by state or national boundaries. After the seed was planted, the movement gained momentum through its significant celebrations: World Day of Prayer, World Community Day, May Fellowship Day (now May Friendship Day), and Human Rights Day.

In the World Day of Prayer Celebration, the women studied, contemplated the scriptures, heard God's word, prayed for guidance, and were moved to advocacy. During May Friendship Day, the women invited other Christian women to fellowship and study local issues. At World Community Day, the women responded to the suffering and oppression of those in our society and took collective action, in faith.

Historical research, discussion roundtables, and interviews conducted to find answers about Seattle's CWU unit closing indicated that for many years SCWU carried out CWU's mission and worked compassionately and diligently for a world of peace and equality. Their visibility in the community earned them respect and credibility not only in Seattle, but also throughout the State of Washington, and the nation. Study revealed that the officers and members of SCWU became aged, fatigued, and discouraged. Additionally, the women did not contact national CWU, the regional coordinator, or the state officers to seek assistance.

Failure to provide a standard SCWU meeting time and venue (preferably a church) was also a factor that weakened SCWU. The women needed a sense of community and better relationships with denominational pastors. Another missed opportunity was SCWU's failure to strategize and hold planning sessions on ways to increase the membership and recruit younger women.

Seven of the fourteen individuals queried about the closure spoke of societal value changes and shifts in Seattle's population demographics. A wealthier citizenry from Microsoft and employees from other corporations that moved to Seattle contributed to the gentrification of the area. Although SCWU had a well-earned reputation for maintaining an integrated unit, because of the city's gentrification, Seattle became re-segregated. This made it difficult for SCWU to retain the racial and economic diversity for which it was known.

Historically, CWU was a religious experience for the generation that created it. Now, it is clearer that each generation must take up the task of discovering ways in which to serve God and humanity.

Two Articles in national CWU's By-laws provide guidelines for unit closures:

> Article XIII. Accountability. Section 1: Local Units, states that: The local units share financial resources and shall provide an annual financial report to the State Treasurer within fifteen (15) days following its Annual meeting of the Leader's Council.

> Article XIV. Dissolution. Section 1: Local Units, states that: In case of dissolution of a local unit, all monies held in the treasury, in the bank and all

accounts must be forwarded to the national office prior to the dissolution.

No one interviewed responded that they were aware of National CWU's provisions for dissolving a local unit.

The opportunity for SCWU Christian women to be together ecumenically still remains; however, according to the women interviewed, only at ecumenical events and interfaith worship service experiences. When interviewed, Dr. Janice Cate stated, "I do not think there are many metropolitan areas where CWU would be relevant because ecumenical leadership is not a priority with the women's departments in denominations."[168]

As current and future generations assess their values, commitment to social justice, and faith in God, the task of learning and understanding who they are in Christ—and their relationship to humanity—will determine whether ecumenical efforts will continue as in the past. What is known is that community is key, and the Spirit moves as it will. A strong prayer life will determine how well women listen and act on what the Spirit is saying to the churches. As this chapter closes, some concluding thoughts and recommendations consider critical points that should be implemented by groups desiring success.

Conclusion

If we pause for a moment to consider CWU as a tapestry, it is obvious that many vertical and horizontal threads are needed to create a tapestry of substance, durability, and vibrancy. The dynamics mentioned earlier in this chapter, namely, sociological, cultural, and theological realities, might be the vertical threads that support the horizontal threads used by the weaver to build her design. In relation to CWU, the horizontal threads could be considered as the good works, service, and prayers, offered on behalf of others, but the weaver must consider the shape, texture, and design of the work being produced. Lack of attention to any aspect of the weaving process results in a tapestry that is something other than the original design.

It was possible that SCWU lost sight of its history and heritage. In former years SCWU's story was one of faith and commitment. The Christian values of the older women were handed down to younger Christian women, who were often their daughters and family members. Involvement in the movement was a spiritual experience that flowed from their love for God, faith in Jesus Christ, and submission to the leading of the Holy Spirit.

During the years prior to SCWU's closure there was failed leadership due to the women's weariness, age, and lack of connectedness to the state and national units. For example, two women who were questioned about the closure indicated that the president and treasurer resigned and the vice-president refused to ascend to the presidency. No mention was made of a secretary who may have resigned earlier. Complicating matters, no minutes existed to document what actually transpired. Unit officers did not take the initiative to contact the national CWU officers, regional, or state leaders. Likewise, they did not review national CWU By-laws regarding unit dissolution.

Keys to Effective Leadership

According to Leonard Doohan, the effective spiritual leader is always reflecting on the past, grasping the values of the present, and looking to the future. Leaders must generate awareness and acceptance of the purpose and mission of their organization and look beyond their own self-interest for the good of the movement. The Christian leader also gives importance to God-directed values. Thus, three essential parts are key to Christian leadership . . . "(1) rootedness: the perennial values must always be the same; (2) interpretation: core values need to always be lived with the same spirit and life often requiring

95

articulation to change in order for the historical essence to remain; and (3) discovery: an attitude of constant openness to the spirit's challenge to each generation."[169]

In spite of SCWU's recent failures, the members must be acknowledged for their many years of outstanding service. Some of the women began when they were young and grew old as they carried out SCWU's mission. Motivated by selfless service to others, SCWU was on the cutting edge of social justice advocacy and peace building. The women demonstrated, spoke, and wrote with fervor and boldness against systemic institutional oppression.

Seattle still honors SCWU's women because their work left an indelible print in the hearts and minds of those whose lives they touched. There were several organizations and activists who were distressed at the loss of SCWU. These include the Church Council of Greater Seattle's Board of Directors, on which presidents of SCWU served for many years, numerous denominational women, community activists, and social justice community-based organizations.

Nevertheless, according to Marilyn Lariviere, CWU National President, "the problem of connecting the National Board with the local units is an ongoing issue. The connection occurs when we have knowledgeable and committed individuals in leadership at all levels.. She further stated, "clearly our system of state and regional leadership is lacking in many areas—we need to be in touch with local units so that when they are struggling (such as was the Seattle Unit), there can be some support available."[170]

If support is not available, one would expect other closures. The national CWU office data recently disclosed that the number of CWU units throughout the nation and Puerto Rico has dropped from 1,000 to approximately 800. Data regarding a final count of active state units and where they are located is not available. The Washington and Northern Idaho CWU State

President, Jeannine Lish, believes that CWU units have fallen to approximately seven although there are two inactive units that are considering starting up again. It may well be that there is a downward trend to active units, of which SCWU was a forerunner.

Impacts When Leadership Ignores Current Realities

Challenges faced by Seattle's CWU unit are not dissimilar from those facing our nation. It is a matter of scale. Our nation is in a state of social, political, and economic change. We face a shrinking middle-class, increased unemployment, blatant racism, and the reality that thousands of women and children are living in poverty. Accordingly, the times we live in require CWU's historical grass roots movement of Christian Unity and prayerful action by women who are impassioned by the Holy Spirit to advocate for those who are suffering, especially women and children. Where do we start? Which loose threads do we strengthen or repair?

The issues facing our nation today have to do with the imbalance of power and wealth, the absence of true democracy, and the political influence needed to correct inequality and the inequities that are so prevalent. Why? Because the benefits of progress are only reaching some sectors of society. Those who are not progressing live with poverty, crime, and fear of premature death if the health system fails. Good health, for example, is influenced by its social and environmental context. Increased life expectancy occurs with every step up the social and economic ladder. Moreover, recently there has been a shift in power. The social and political wealthy majority, living in gentrified cities, has caused minority populations to experience a post-modern diaspora as they move to other less expensive cities where they have very little political or economic power.

Racism

Blatant racism is on the rise. Few individuals will admit they have any racial prejudices. Yet, they choose to believe stereotypes rather than accept evidence contradictory to what they have been taught. Those individuals who learn the facts come face to face with who they are as human beings and how they relate to those who differ in culture and/or skin color.

Politics and our national government also play a role in perpetuating racism. Never in the history of this nation has the office of the President of the United States been so disrespected by Republican and Democratic Congressmen and -women in both houses. President Barak Obama's race was a hot topic used to distract citizens from the deep work of democracy, while the mass media right-wing talk-show pundits continue to fan the flames by propagating racial stereotypes.

Moreover, personal and institutional racism has played a role in the distribution of wealth in the United States. Discrimination against racial and ethnic minorities, lower incomes, fewer job opportunities and growing patterns of structural injustice take root—and are sustained by a sleeping majority. At present, the U.S. Constitution is being challenged by states' rights proponents who propose voting eligibility requirements that will affect the under-educated, the elderly, and ultimately turn the clock back to voter suppression, state rights, and Jim Crow laws.

Educational Issues

Our educational system presents two faces to society. One face is that it is our most important democratic institutional pathway to class mobility and generational progress; however, its failure to graduate all young people impacts the prospects of millions of families and children every day. The other face of our educational system reinforces the class and race privilege for those who can afford the increasing costs of higher education.

To compound matters, the United States Supreme Court on June 28, 2007, in Parents Involved in Community Schools vs. the Seattle School District, ruled that public school systems cannot seek to achieve or maintain integration through measures that take explicit account of a student's race—thereby re-segregating public school systems. According to Justice Stevens, the justices limited the use of race in school plans for integration. The majority opinion rewrote the history of one of the Court's most important decisions by ignoring the context in which Brown was issued. The 2007 ruling was in direct contrast to the principles of the Brown vs. the Board of Education's landmark case in 1954 (*New York Times* published June 29, 2007).

Washington State also has its problems. On January 5, 2012, the State Supreme Court ruled in McCleary v. Washington that Washington State is not amply funding basic education under the state Constitution.... The Washington State Constitution, Article IX: Section 1, *Preamble* states the following: "It is the paramount duty of the state to make ample provision for the education for all children residing within its borders, without distinction or preference on account of race, color, caste, or sex." In other words it is the duty of the state to provide ample financial support for basic education." (Washington State OSPI). For the first time in history, on September 24, 2014, the Washington Supreme Court held state legislators in contempt for failing to obey a court order. Therefore, if lawmakers fail to develop a funding plan by the end of the 2015 legislative session, the court signaled it might act swiftly to punish them.

Today, CWU units have an opportunity to speak out against these atrocities that breach community and family values. Will the women of CWU continue the legacy of courage and fortitude? Have the recommendations submitted to CWU (see Appendix B) been considered and implemented? In light of the great shifts occurring in society, can the tapestry be mended and restored? Only time will tell.

My prayer is that God will grant CWU the love, courage, and vitality to continue for decades; however, it must unite through the inspiration and fire of the Holy Spirit to uphold justice and *visibly stand against poverty and racism* in our nation. The Wisdom of Solomon in the book of Ecclesiastes Chapter 3:1 reminds us that "To everything there is a season, and a time to every purpose under heaven." Now, more than ever before, is the season for Christians to stand against poverty and racism—to weave their lives of faith around providing sorely needed social justice.

TOPICS FOR DISCUSSION

- What is meant by the culture of amnesia and how does it influence an organization?

- How does a crisis of leadership occur and what happens after it occurs?

- How does an organization's mission become compromised?

- What impact or role has "gentrification" had on integration and the balance of wealth?

- What can be done to address the issue of institutional and personal racism and poverty?

GLOSSARY

Key terms are defined here to aid the reader:

Ecumenism is a noun which came from the Greek word "oikoumene," meaning the unity of the whole inhabited world (Matt. 24:14). Gradually the term came to refer to the whole Christian church as opposed to that which is divided. It covers equally the missionary movement and the movement toward unity.

Ecumenical Movement. The movement between Christian churches in the twentieth and twenty-first centuries seeking visible unity and renewal.

Liberation Theology "develops the meaning of the Gospel of Jesus Christ as historically liberative. Faith is the formal starting point, the word of God is the objective faith, the perspective of the poor and oppressed is the subjective faith. The practice of faith includes themes of oppression and liberation." [171]

Movements are characterized by faith, commitment to a cause, rapid mobilization and adaptive methods. In the case of CWU, "The movement was a living faith in God and each other that bound Christian women together."[172]

Praxis is an established custom or habitual practice as in Church Women United's praxis of prayer, reflection, power, and prophetic action.

Social Gospel is the application of Christian social principles and Jesus' message to the problems of society that are perpetrated by social and economic systems that oppress the weak.[173]

Social Justice is associated with righteousness and non-partiality within societal institutions and systems governing a society.

The term *unit* was adopted by CWU to define a local, state, or regional area operating under its own by-laws that are in harmony with national CWU's purpose.[174]

ENDNOTES

Preface

[1.] Iva E. Caruthers, "Called to be the Salt of the Earth, In Hopkins, Dwight N., and Linda E. Thomas, eds. 2009. Walk together children: Black and womanist theologies, church and theological education. Eugene, Oregon: Wipf & Stock Publishers.

Introduction

[2.] Arleon L. Kelly, ed. 2004. A tapestry of justice, service, and unity: Local ecumenism in the United States, 1950–2000. Tacoma, WA: National Association of Ecumenical and Interreligious Staff Press.

[3.] Margaret Shannon, Carolyn L. Stang, and Billie Ann Wilson. 1977. Just because: The story of the national movement of Church Women United in the U.S.A., 1941–1975. Corte Madera, CA: Omega Books.

[4.] Martha Lee Wiggins. 2005. United Church Women: A constant drip of water will wear a hole in iron: The ecumenical struggle of church women to unite across race and shape the civil rights century. PhD Dissertation, Union Theological Seminary.

[5.] Church Women United. 2004. Basic Book. Rev. ed. New York: Church Women United National Office.

[6.] Janice Cate. Interview with author. Seattle, WA February 2011.

Chapter One

[7.] Shannon, Stang, and Wilson, 1977. Just Because.

[8.] Shannon, Stang, and Wilson, 1977. Just Because, 5.

[9.] Shannon, Stang, and Wilson. 1977, Just because, 6.

[10.] Shannon, Stang, and Wilson. 1977, Just because, 7.

[11.] Shannon, Stang, and Wilson. 1977, Just because.

[12.] Shannon, Stang, and Wilson. 1977, Just because, 7.

[13.] Shannon, Stang, and Wilson. 1977, Just because, 8.

[14.] Ibid.

[15.] Ibid.

[16.] Ibid.

[17.] Shannon, Stang, and Wilson. 1977, Just because, 6.

[18.] CWU Basic Book 2004, 10.

[19.] Shannon, Stang, and Wilson. 1977, Just because, 8.

[20.] Shannon, Stang, and Wilson. 1977, Just because.

[21.] CWU Basic Book 2004, 10.

[22.] Shannon, Stang, and Wilson. 1977, Just because, 10.

[23.] Shannon, Stang, and Wilson 1977.

[24.] Church Women United 2001, Souvenir Memory Book. 1869-2001. New York: Church Women United National Office, 229.

[25.] CWU 2004 Basic Handbook.

[26.] CWU 2001 Souvenir Memory Book, 27.

[27.] CWU 2001 Souvenir Memory Book, 26.

[28.] Howard Zinn. 1995. A people's history of the United States: 1942-present. New York: Harper Perennial.

[29.] Shannon, Stang, and Wilson 1977.

[30.] Shannon, Stang, and Wilson 1977, 4.

[31.] Ibid.

[32.] Kelly 2004, A Tapestry, 75.

[33.] Shannon, Stang, and Wilson 1977.

[34.] CWU 2001, Souvenir Memory Book, 3.

[35.] Shannon, Stang, and Wilson 1977.

[36.] CWU 2001, Souvenir Memory Book 2001.

[37.] Janice Cate 1991, 8.

[38.] Janice Cate 1991, 6.

[39.] Davidson Nicol, UNITARnews, 1975, 3.

[40.] Kelly 2007, A tapestry, 75.

[41.] Martha Lee Wiggins 2005, United Church Women: A constant, 111–113.

[42.] Martha Lee Wiggins 2005.

[43.] Ibid.

[44.] Kelly 2004, A tapestry.

Chapter Two

[45.] Kelly 2004, A tapestry, 79.

[46.] CWU 2004 Basic Book, 14.

[47.] CWU 2004 Basic Book.

[48.] Shannon, Stang, and Wilson 1977, 178.

Chapter Three

[49.] Church Women United. 2003. Social Policies. 1941–2003, New York: Church Women United National Office, 95–96.

[50.] Christian Century, 1961, "UCW to campaign against racism," Christian Century, 78 no. 43: ATLA Religion Database with ATLA Serials, EBSCO Host (accessed June 29, 2010), 126.

[51.] Christian Century,1962, "Churchwomen lay faith on line." Christian Century, 316 (March 14). ATLA Religion Database with ATLA Serials, EBSCO Host (accessed June 29, 2010).

[52.] Shannon, Stang, and Wilson, 1977. Just Because.

[53.] Shannon, Stang, and Wilson. 1977, Just because, 119.

[54.] Richard C. Remy 1990. Government in the United States. Mission Hills, CA: Glencoe, 71.

[55.] Zinn 1995, A people's history, 447.

[56.] Http://millercenter.org/presidentlbjohnson/essays/biography/4

[57.] Kelly 2004, A tapestry, 85.

[58.] Shannon, Stang and Wilson, 1977, Just because, 278.

[59.] Kelly 2004, A tapestry.

[60.] Shannon, Stang and Wilson, 1977, Just because, 287.

[61.] Shannon, Stang and Wilson, 1977, Just because, 225.

[62.] Shannon, Stang and Wilson, 1977, Just because, 416–17.

[63.] Zinn 1995, A people's history.

[64.] Shannon, Stang and Wilson, 1977, Just because, 281.

[65.] Milton C. Cummings, Jr. and David Wise, 1997. Democracy under pressure: An introduction to the American political system. Eighth Ed. Fort Worth, TX: Harcourt Brace & Company, 62.

[66.] Zinn 1995, A people's history, 530.

[67.] Zinn 1995, A people's history, 559.

[68.] Zinn 1995, A people's history.

[69.] .Kelly 2004, A tapestry.

[70.] Zinn 1995, A people's history, 565.

[71.] Zinn 1995, A people's history, 569.

[72.] CWU Policy Statement on Hunger, 1995, 79.

[73.] Shannon, Stang and Wilson, 1977, Just because.

[74.] Brun 1997, 50.

[75.] CWU. 2003. Social Policies 1941–2003, New York: Church Women United National Office, 138.

[76.] Zinn 1995, A people's history, 631.

[77.] CWU 2003. Social Policies, 1993, 239.

[78.] Brun 1997, 53.

[79.] Brun 1997.

[80.] CWU Basic Book.

[81.] CWU 2003, Social Policies. Sec XXVII (28), 105–106.

[82.] CWU 2004, Resolution Israel/Palestine, 106–108.

[83.] CWU 2008, Resolution Israel/Palestine, 196.

Chapter Four

[84.] Shannon, Stang and Wilson, 1977, Just because, 175.

[85.] Kelly 2004, A Tapestry

108

86. Centennial Ecumenical Gathering. 2010. "Studies 2010: Christian understanding of Unity in an age of radical diversity." Paper presented at the Centennial Ecumenical Gathering, New Orleans, LA. November 9–11.

87. Michael Kinnamon and Brian E. Cope. 1997. The ecumenical movement: An anthology of key texts and voices. Geneva, Switzerland: World Council of Churches.

88. Kinnamon and Cope 1997, 5.

89. Kinnamon and Cope, 1997.

90. Kinnamon and Cope, 4.

91. William Cate. 1985. "The local church as a new theology of ecumenism." The Source, vol. 9 (March 8). Seattle, WA. Church Council of Greater Seattle, 7.

92. World Council of Churches, Faith and Order Commission, Paper 111, 1982.

93. Kinnamon and Cope, 1997.

94. Intro to Theology in an Ecumenical context 1993, 3–4.

95. Crawford, Janet Estridge. 1995. Rocking the Boat: Women's participation in the World Council of Churches 1948–1991. PhD Dissertation, Victoria University of Wellington, 48.

96. World Council of Churches, 1948.

97. Crawford 1995, 370.

98. Crawford 1995, 253.

99. Centennial Ecumenical Gathering. 2010. "Studies 2010: Christian understanding of Unity in an age of radical diversity." Paper presented at the Centennial Ecumenical Gathering. New Orleans, LA. November, 9–11, 7.

100. James Forbes. Interview with the author. Seattle, WA. February, 2011, 1.

Chapter Five

101. Elsie M. Boulding. 1976. The underside of history: A view of women through time. New York: Halsted.

[102.] Jessie K. Kenton. 2000. Church Women United in the Seattle area: Unpublished manuscript. Washington State Women's History Archive, Tacoma, WA.

[103.] Kenton, 2000, 4.

[104.] Kenton. 2000.

[105.] Ibid.

[106.] Kenton, 2000, 8.

[107.] Kenton 2000.

[108.] Ibid.

[109.] Ibid.

[110.] Kenton, 31.

[111.] Kenton, 31-32.

[112.] Kenton. 2000, 32.

[113.] Kenton 2000.

[114.] Ibid.

[115.] Ibid.

[116.] Photographs of Jeraldine Bright, Janice Cate, and Jean Kim, circa 1981, are courtesy of The Church Council of Greater Seattle which holds the rights to The Source newspaper, which is no longer published.

[117.] The Source, 1983, 5.

[118.] Ibid.

[119.] Kenton. 2000, 47.

[120.] Cate, 1991.

[121.] Ibid.

[122.] Penny Poor. 1983. "CWU to monitor emergency rooms." The Source, no. 5 (January). Seattle, WA: Church Council of Greater Seattle, 4.

[123.] Kenton. 2000.

[124.] Ibid.

125. CWU Social Policies 1941–2003, 1983, 139.

126. Kenton. 2000.

127. Zinn 1995, A people's history.

128. Phyllis Beaumonte. 1982. "Nuclear arms cause crisis of faith." The Source. vol. 7. (December), 4. Seattle, WA: Church Council of Greater Seattle.

129. The Source. 1987. "Infant formula campaign continues: Infant health campaign," The Source. vol. 11, no. 7, 4. (March). Seattle, WA: Church Council of Greater Seattle.

130. Mae Schaefer, 1988, "Assignment: Poverty of Women. *The Source*, vol. 13, no. 1. (February), Seattle, WA: Church Council of Greater Seattle.

131. Schaefer 1988,4.

132. Shelly Anderson n.d., Overview of Women in black. http://www.scn.org/womeninblack/about.htm (accessed June 2010), 1.

133. Anderson, n.d.

134. Jan Cate 2011.

135. Author's personal experience.

136. CWU Basic Book Revised 2004.

Chapter Six

137. CWU Basic Book 2004, By-Laws, 1.

138. Ignacio Ellacuria, S.J. and Jon Sobrino, S.J. eds. 1993 Mysterium liberationis: Fundamental concepts of liberation theology. Maryknoll, NY: Orbis Books.

139. James E. Tull. 1984. Shapers of Baptist thought. Macon, GA: Mercer University Press.

140. Ibid.

141. Remy 1990, Government, 25.

142. Serene Jones and Paul Lakeland, Eds. 2005. Constructive Theology: A contemporary approach to classic themes. Minneapolis, MN: Augsburg Fortress, 180.

143. Walter Rauschenbusch, 1891, Christianity Revolutionary.

144. Walter Rauschenbusch 1964,.Christianity and the social crisis. New York: Harper & Row.

145. Tull 1984, Shapers of Baptist thought.

146. Ibid.

147. Gary Dorrien. 2007. Spiritual leadership: The quest for integrity. New York/Mahwah, NJ: Paulist Press, 2.

148. Tull 1984, Shapers of Baptist thought.

149. Ibid.

150. Tull 1984, Shapers of Baptist thought, 193.

151. Alfred T. Hennelly, S.J. 1997. Liberation theologies: The global pursuit of justice. Mystic, CT: Twenty-Third Publications.

152. Philip Potter. 1981. Life in all its fullest. Geneva, Switzerland: World Council of Churches, 150.

153. Ellacuria and Sobrino. 1993.

154. Placido Erdozain. 1981. Archbishop Romero, martyr of Salvador. Maryknoll, NY: Orbis Books.

155. Shannon 1977.

156. Debra B. Hull. 2008, "Mossie Allman Wyker: Ordained to change the world." Discipliana, 67, no. 12 (March 1, 2008) 3–25: ATLA Religion Database with ATLA Serials, EBSCO host (accessed June 29, 2010).

157. Mossie A. Wyker. 1953. Church women in the scheme of things. Columbia. MO: Bethany Press, 7.

158. Wyker 1953.

159. Ibid.

160. Hull. 2008.

161. Tull 1984, Shapers of Baptist thought.

162. Tull 1984, Shapers of Baptist thought, 220.

163. King, Martin Luther, Jr. 1986. Letter from a Birmingham Jail, In King: The making of a legend, ed. Gary Puckrein, 52-29.

164. Tull 1984, Shapers of Baptist thought, 216.

165. Coretta Scott King. 1993. The Martin Luther King, Jr. companion. New York: St. Martin's Press.

166. Tull, 1984, Shapers of Baptist thought, 232.

167. Ibid.

Chapter Eight

168. Jan Cate interview with author, 2011.

169. Leonard Doohan. 2007. Spiritual leadership: The quest for integrity. New York/Mahwah, NJ, 115.

170. Marilyn Lariviere, personal communication with the author

Glossary

171. Ellacuria & Sobrino 1993, 57.

172. Shannon, Stang and Wilson, 1977, Just because, 4.

173. Tull 1984, Shapers of Baptist thought.

174. Shannon, Stang and Wilson, 1977, Just because.

113

APPENDIX A

FOUR OPTIONS FOR CWU INVOLVEMENT

Option One: Church Women United Local Unit:

Expectations of the Local Unit:

- A local unit observes all three celebrations and sends report forms to national and state.
- A local unit accepts the Common Goals of Church Women United.
- A local unit has functional relationship with state and national units of Church Women United in the development and implementation of national program priorities.
- A local unit financially supports the work of state and national units through World Day of Prayer, World Community Day offerings, purchase of Church Women United resources, and general contributions to the ongoing work of Church Women United.
- A local unit has an organization adequate to meet its goals; informs the national and state unit through the return for the annual local unit officer form; and of any additional changes.

Expectations of the State Unit:

- The state unit incorporates the local unit into the state unit through newsletters, area contacts, state assemblies and other activities as appropriate.

Expectations of the National Unit:

- The national office sends a sample packet of Celebrations materials to the local president yearly.

- The national organization gives a *Church Woman News* subscription to the local unit president.

- The national office sends the local president materials appropriate to the local actions and participation related to the national program priorities.

- The national office keeps a local unit officer computer file, will inform the state officers of local unit changes and possibilities for revitalization of existing units or development of new units.

- The national office provides leadership development and personal growth seminars through regional events and state assemblies.

Option Two: Celebrations Unit

Expectations of the Local Unit:

- The Celebrations unit holds two or more Celebration services per year including Bible study of follow-up action.
- The Celebrations unit returns Celebrations report forms and offerings to the national office and a copy to the State Celebration Coordinator following each celebration.
- The Celebration unit identifies a contact person for the community for all Celebrations.

Expectations of the State unit:

- The state unit gives assistance to units requesting help in forming a CWU local unit.
- The state unit informs units through newsletters and other appropriate activities.

Expectations of the National Unit:

- The national unit assigns an identification number to each Celebration unit.
- The national unit sends each unit contact person the annual sample celebration packet.
- The national unit responds to a unit requesting information on forming a CWU local unit.
- The national unit sends an annual report to the Celebration unit.

Option Three: World Day of Prayer Unit

Expectations of the World Day of Prayer Unit:

- The World Day of Prayer unit celebrates World Day of Prayer.
- The World Day of Prayer unit returns a Celebrations form and the offering to the Church Women United national office.
- The World Day of Prayer unit indicates the person to receive the order form for the next year.

Expectations of the State unit:

- The state unit responds with assistance to World Day of Prayer units requesting help in forming a Church Women United or a Celebrations unit.

Expectations of the National Unit:

- The national office receives the celebrations report and offering and acknowledges same.
- The national office sends an order-form mailing to the person designated to receive it.
- The national office responds to requests for information on forming a Church Women United local unit or Celebrations unit.
- The national unit informs the state unit of request for assistance in becoming a Church Women United local unit or Celebrations unit.
- The national unit sends an annual report to each World Day of Prayer unit.

Option Four: Church Women United Affiliate Unit

Expectations of the Church Women United Affiliate Unit:

- A group of women indicates interest in Church Women United.
- A group of women, may gather to further a Church Women United national program priority and/or implement Church Women United goals and/or discuss an issue pertinent to Church Women United national priorities in a variety of non-traditional settings (e.g. college campus; prison; seminary; work place; community center, etc.)
- A group of women will express their ecumenical solidarity and will be receptive to Church Women United informational materials.
- A group of women will participate where possible in Celebrations with other units.

Expectations of the State Unit:

- The state acknowledges interest from a potential Church Women United Affiliate by responding to an individual or a CWU local unit with options or suggestions, as appropriate.
- The state unit informs the national unit of the interest expressed for a Church Women United Affiliate.

Expectations of the National Unit:

- The national unit acknowledges interest from a potential Church Women United affiliate by responding to an individual or a Church women United local unit with options or suggestions as appropriate.
- The national unit informs the state unit and the appropriate local unit or metro-group of the interest expressed for a Church Women United affiliate unit.

The Criteria and Options for CWU Units are found in *Church Women United Basic Book*, Revised February 2004, 12–13.

APPENDIX B

RECOMMENDATIONS SUBMITTED

TO NATIONAL CWU

Recommendations

Based on the author's findings, the following recommendations were prayerfully submitted to the national, regional, and state units of CWU:

- That national CWU review its by-laws to include more reporting procedures and checks and balances (accountability) regarding the responsibilities of local units to the state and national units.
- That national CWU design a brochure to disseminate describing the opportunity for young Christian women to enhance their skills and professional experience while serving Christ and empowering others.
- That all local unit officers and members subscribe to the *ChurchWoman News*, the official organ of CWU, in order to stay informed.
- That national CWU prioritize at least one local social justice issue for all local units to work on simultaneously to increase the visibility, impact, and success of CWU's efforts.
- That national CWU provide training on an ongoing basis for local unit officers, members, and new members.
- That national CWU and local units convey the significance of CWU's history and mission to inspire potential members, particularly younger women.
- That national CWU formulate a policy to enable local units to establish partnerships with local seminaries and explore the possibility of

providing academic credits for students who work with CWU.

- That national CWU encourage local units to accommodate working women with either night or week-end meetings.
- That national CWU promote the involvement of local units with local ecumenical Church Councils.
- That national CWU require all units to implement the Young CWU Initiative and report regularly to national CWU on the results of their efforts.

APPENDIX C

COMMENTARIES

COMMENTARIES

An Apology, and Acceptance Would Mend Some Wounds

Printed in The Seattle Post-Intelligencer, April 25, 1998

The question of whether President Clinton, on behalf of the nation, should apologize for slavery was responded to recently in an April 7 article by Thomas Geoghegan.

According to Geoghegan, "What's so strange or scary is that an apology would drop out of our heads. What is the reason, I wonder"? The answer is found within the psyche of most white Americans who believe in their racial superiority, which is a form of racism.

That slavery was a necessary evil, which evolved for the economic success of the South, made it all right for the white colonists to give no concern in the cultural deprivation and the demoralization of the African slave's human dignity. When African slaves fought in the American Revolutionary War and every subsequent war on behalf of this country, it was also of no consequence regarding their liberty. Identified by their skin color, the stigma of being "black" in this country, then and now, continues within racist connotations to represent everything evil and inferior. Those myths and stereotypes are a real part of America's value system, and the extreme psychological damage from those ungodly practices will continue to affect African Americans.

Whether it is necessary to apologize to African Americans for slavery must be answered within the context of how the historical phenomenon is perceived by society today. There are implications that African Americans are still the recipients of racist ideologies that evolved during and after the time of slavery. The federal government, after passing the 14th Amendment to the Constitution, giving equal protection under the law to citizens, allowed the states to enforce Jim Crow laws that relegated African Americans to second-class citizen-ships that continued for decades. As a result, lynchings and killings of African Americans went unchecked for years.

Today, many white teens are violent toward African Americans and other people of color. There are educational systems that allow textbooks and instruction to propagate negative stereotypes that evolved during the slavery period. Go into any number of public places and you will find racial epithets scrawled on walls. African Americans, more than any other race, are harassed by police officers.

The answer is yes, there needs to be a public apology and acknowledgment by this nation that slavery was wrong, as a first step in a long overdue healing process.

Forgiveness, being the clearest evidence of the power of love, must be given by African Americans when the apology is extended. Forgiveness can bring reconciliation rather than estrangement and reunion rather than fear and hostility.

Phyllis R. Beaumonte

Seattle

Dismantling Racism and White Privilege: An Elusive Goal

Phyllis Ilene Ratcliff-Beaumonte

Published in *The Source,* February 2001, 5

White racism is the teaching that one racial group is inferior and another is destined to hereditary superiority. It has been historically supported and in some cases aided by white religion. Consequently, the theory of white supremacy has been maintained in spite of efforts to build an authentic just society.

When I first read and heard the words "dismantling white privilege," I felt concerned regarding the connotations that would evolve from using that term, primarily because many white Americans believe they should be privileged.

Certainly, this subject will be discussed over lunches, forums, and dinner engagements by various church groups and community dialogues; however, unless there is an honest reevaluation and revolution of values and beliefs, which are deeply ingrained in white America's psyche, progress to dismantle racism and white privilege will be superficial. Traditional values often create conflict between those who yearn and struggle to participate in real change and share power with those who seek to maintain the status quo.

Christians more so than others must shift back from secular to religious values; a shift from the comfort of tradition (accepting situation ethics as a standard) to obedience to God. Philip Potter, former general secretary of the World Council of Churches, wrote in his book *Life in Its Fullness* "the Christian duty is to express solidarity with the oppressed in all ways compatible with our faith and in recognition of our own solidarity against the sin of racism.

The churches, as an expression of the body of Christ and as servant of people who participate in the life of their societies, often participate in the racist system either by active involvement or by passive complicity."

Today, white racism and oppression in America is institutionalized through various policies, systems, and government. Examples include racial profiling, which is prevalent in many aspects of daily living, the unequal disbursement of resources throughout our educational system, unfair sentencing laws for drug crimes, questionable justifiable police shootings, and alleged excessive force used by some police officers. These oppressive factors are evidence that although some progress has been made, racism is still very active in America. We have a long way to go.

Conversely, God's righteousness, as seen through the ministry and teaching of Jesus Christ and expressed through His compassion and action, is based on the reality of His deliverance of the oppressed from the shackles of human bondage. In Jesus Christ, all people regardless of race, sex, caste, or ethnic descent are reconciled to God and to each other. Therefore, "racism as an ideology and discrimination as a practice are a betrayal of the rich diversity of God's design for the world and violate the dignity of human personality." All forms of racism, whether individual, collective or systemic must be named sin. Let us encourage all Christians regardless of color to continue the struggle for justice for all oppressed people.

Promises of Brown v. Board unfulfilled

Phyllis Beaumonte: Seattle Post-Intelligencer guest columnist

May 31, 2004

Gradually, it is becoming clearer that the problems of inequities in public education are becoming more complex and urgent. Fifty years after the Brown v. Board of Education decision, although some progress has been made, prevalent and persistent inequities in our nation's public education system indicate the Brown promise remains unfulfilled, and the system is substantively still separate and still unequal.

Earlier this month, I was one of about 100 NAACP state education chairs and education specialists who attended the NAACP Education Summit of States in Topeka, Kansas. The Summit coincided with the anniversary of the Brown decision, in which the U.S. Supreme Court declared separate but equal schooling unconstitutional.

The Summit's purpose was to present the "Brown Fifty Years and Beyond: Promise and Progress Advocacy Report," which focused on the goal of ensuring all students have access to a high-quality integrated education in the 21st century.

According to NAACP national officials it is not only *de jure* segregation but *de facto* segregation of students today that perpetuates an educational environment that is "inherently unequal." The issue is separate and unequal access to resources in public education resulting from systemic institutionalized racism that impacts children of color and white students.

- Teachers in high-poverty, high-minority areas are more often poorly trained in curriculum and

133

instruction, classroom management and cultural sensitivity.

- Neighborhoods remain segregated, which contributes to highly segregated schools.

- School data, when disaggregate, show racial achievement gaps in learning.

- Minority students are more often assigned to low track and special education than white students.

- Minority students have fewer opportunities to take advanced "gatekeeper" courses required for post-secondary education.

- Minority students are more frequently suspended or expelled and are more likely to enter the juvenile justice system through a school-to-prison pipeline.

- Underfunded schools are deprived of basic materials, support services and adequate counseling.

- Hundreds of children enter public education without having the experience of Head Start and early childhood training, which puts them at an academic disadvantage.

These issues have gone unchecked for quite some time. However, in 2001 the NAACP asked federal, state and local educational agencies to design and implement a five-tier educational equity partnership plan to reduce disparities by 50 percent and to submit their plans to the NAACP in May 2002. Governor Gary Locke and Superintendent of Public Instruction, Terry Bergeson submitted a plan.

Subsequently, at the Topeka Summit, a "Call for Action" five-year-plan template was presented. The template is to be used by states to begin implementing their plans and report yearly progress, beginning with the year 2005 and ending in 2009. The template, soon to be distributed to governors and education superintendents, will be monitored by NAACP state education chairs throughout the nation, as well as the national NAACP.

The Brown court provided unprecedented moral as well as political leadership by reminding the nation through its ruling that the Constitution applies to all American. Brown stripped our country of the double standards imposed upon African Americans through the "separate but equal doctrine."

Now, however, we must look to our states and their school districts to rise to the moral challenge of providing equity and equality in resources and public policies so every child has equal access to a quality and integrated education. The state has, by law, undertaken the responsibility to provide an opportunity for an education in its public schools. Such an opportunity is a right that must be made available to all on equal terms. For the state to allow inequity in the application of public policies that breed segregation and discrimination in school districts denies the rights of it citizens.

We cannot have two educational systems. Lack of opportunity for a quality integrated education will prove to be a casualty that will continue to burden our state and nation. Equity in educational resources and quality teachers will enable and encourage all students to achieve their best. Parental and guardian responsibility, accountability and spiritual

135

empowerment are equally as important in contributing to a child's success and must not be discounted. A common commitment can create the climate in which solutions are possible.

Stereotyping Persists

by Phyllis R. Beaumonte – Special to *The Seattle Times*

Printed in *The Seattle Times* on October 15, 2005

The first Amendment is designed particularly to protect ideas that may be unpopular or different from our own. Justice Oliver Wendell Holmes said democracy required not only freedom of speech for those who agree with us, but also "freedom for the thought we hate."

Citizens in a democracy also have a right to hear and judge for themselves what others have to say. That right compelled me to respond to the former U.S. Secretary of Education William Bennett's remarks regarding aborting black babies to reduce the crime rate.

Bennett told a caller to his syndicated radio talk show recently: "If you wanted to reduce crime, you could—if that was your sole purpose—you could abort every black baby in this country and your crime rate would go down." He further stated, "that would be an impossibly ridiculous and morally reprehensible thing to do, but your crime rate would go down."

Here is the spin. Bennett claimed that he was not advocating his supposition and when asked if he owed people an apology, he replied, "I don't think I do. I think people who misrepresented my view owe me an apology."

One would think that a scholar of Bennett's stature would be too prudent and intelligent to present a theory predicated on a racial stereotype—even within a hypothetical context. His statement was an expression of his belief that all black babies grow up to become criminals: a prejudgment of black children.

On the other hand, people who stereotype, such as Bennett, may not always realize that is what they are doing. They learn to accept negative qualities that are found within a race and ignore anything to the contrary.

When this happens, a person will eventually form a personal conviction that prejudging African Americans, for example, is the right and acceptable way to think.

Equally tragic is his lack of sensitivity for the value of life for black babies. God has a very special love for all humankind, especially babies and children regardless of race, color, or creed. They are all precious in his sight. To propose, even in theory, the genocide of black babies through abortion is evil and incomprehensible.

APPENDIX D

KEY RESPONSES TO INTERVIEW QUESTIONS REGARDING CLOSURE OF SCWU

Question Three: (A) Why did SCWU decide to close and (B) what protocols were followed?

Participant Responses to Question Three A

Why did SCWU decide to close?

Number of themes most often found in the responses

THEMES	# OF RESPONSES
Answer unknown	5
Societal changes	7
Lack of commitment	6
Poor administration	3
Need for younger women	14
The older women were burned out	14
Lack of communication	3
Other	

Clearly, all the Participants agreed that there was a need to recruit younger women and there were challenges with the aging of SCWU's officers and members. These were the primary reasons for the closure of Seattle Church Women United.

141

Participant Responses to Question Three B What protocols were followed? Number of themes most often found in the responses	
THEMES	# OF RESPONSES
Unaware of protocol	14

Question Four: How was the decision made?

Participant Responses to Question Four How was the decision made? Number of themes most often found in the responses	
THEME	# OF RESPONSES
Respondent did know	1
Respondents did not know	13

The table revealed that only one of the fourteen Participants knew how the decision was made to close Seattle Church Women United.

Question Five: What could have been done, if anything, to save SCWU?

Participant Responses to Question Five What could have been done to save SCWU? Number of themes most often found in the responses	
THEMES	# OF RESPONSES
Need ongoing leadership training from National and the State units	4
Foster commitment to the heritage and mission of CWU	3
Share CWU and SCWU's story with younger women	9
Provide a standard meeting time and place	10
Continue holding meetings in churches	3
Reach out to younger women	14
Recruit new fresh leadership	5
Continue visibility in Seattle	5
Hold strategy sessions and workshops to plan how to increase membership	4

Analysis revealed that Seattle Church Women United could have been a thriving local unit had members recruited younger women, provided a standard meeting time and place, remained visible in the Seattle community, and witnessed to the uniqueness of their historical legacy as a strategy for their recruitment of younger women.

Additionally, roundtables and interview sessions revealed that Seattle Church Women United could have remained active had they continued to communicate and stay connected to national, regional, and state CWU units.

REFERENCES

Anderson, Shelly. n.d. An Overview of Women in Black. http://www.scn.org/womeninblack/about.htm (Accessed June 2010)

Arendt, Hannah. 1961. Between past and future. New York: Viking Press.

Baron, Virginia O. 1978. ,A good day on the urban causeway. Christian Century 95, no.22 (June 21, 1978): 646–648. ATA Religion Database with ATLASerials, EBSCOhost (accessed June 29, 2010).

Beaumonte, Phyllis. 1982. "Nuclear arms cause crisis of faith." The Source. vol.7, (December, 4). Seattle, WA: Church Council of Greater Seattle.

Bellah, Robert N. 1985. Habits of the heart: Individualism and commitment in American life. California: University of California Press.

Boff, Leonardo. 1978. Jesus Christ liberator. Trans. Patrick Hughes. Maryknoll, NY: Orbis Books.

Boff, Leonardo. 1984. Salvation and Liberation. trans. Robert K. Boff. Maryknoll, N.Y: Orbis Books.

Boff, Leonardo and Clodovis Boff. 1987. Introducing liberation theology. Trans. Paul Burns. Tunbridge Wells: Burns and Oates. Maryknoll, N.Y: Orbis Books.

Boulding, Elsie M. 1976. The underside of history: A view of women through time. New York: Halsted.

Brink, William, and Louis Harris. 1963. The Negro revolution in America. New York: Simon and Schuster.

Buerge, David and Junius Rochester. 1988. Roots and branches: The religious heritage of Washington State. Seattle, WA: Church Council of Greater Seattle.

Burton, Jane. 1981. Church women united. Reformed World 36, no. 7 (September 1, 1981): 327–328/ ATLA Religion Database with ATLASerials, EBSCOhost (accessed June 29, 2010. SFTS BX9801.RC.v.36).

Caputo, John D., and Brian McLauren. 2007. What would Jesus deconstruct? The good news of post modernism for the church. Grand Rapids, MI: Baker Academic.

Cate, Janice. 2011. Interview with author. Seattle, WA: February, 2011.

Cate, William. 1985. "The local church as a new theology of ecumenism." The Source, vol. 9 (March 8). Seattle, WA: Church Council of Greater Seattle.

Cate, William. 2011. Interview with author. Seattle, WA: February 2011.

Centennial Ecumenical Gathering. 2010. "Studies 2010: Christian understanding of Unity in an age of radical diversity." Paper presented at the Centennial Ecumenical Gathering, New Orleans, LA. November 9–11.

Charmaz, K. 2003. "Grounded theory: Objectivist and constructivist methods." In Strategies of qualitative inquiry, eds. N.K. Denzin and Y. S. Lincoln. Thousand Oaks, CA: Sage Publications, 249–291.

Christian Century. 1961. "UCW to campaign against racism." Christian Century, 78, no.43: ATLA Religion Database with ATLA Serials, EBSCOHost (accessed June 29, 2010).

Christian Century. 1962. "Churchwomen lay faith on line." Christian Century, 316 (March 14). ATLA Religion Database with ATLA Serials, EBSCOHost (accessed June, 29, 2010).

Church Woman. 1956. "The ecumenical mind." The Church Woman, New York: Church Women United.

Church Women United. 2001. Church Women United Souvenir Memory Book. 1869–2001. New York, NY: Church Women United National Office.

Church Women United. 2003. Social Policies. 1941–2003. New York: Church Women United National Office.

Church Women United. 2004. Basic Book. Rev. ed. New York: Church Women United National Office.

Church Women United. 2005. Social Policies: Resolutions and statements, 2005–2010. New York: Church Women United National Office.

Clark, Kenneth B. 1966. "The Civil Rights Movement: Momentum and organization." Daedalus 95, no.1 (winter): 239–267.

Cleaver, Eldridge. 1968. Soul on ice. New York: Dell.

Cummings, Milton C. Jr., and David Wise.1997. Democracy under pressure: An introduction to the American political system. Eighth Edition. Fort Worth, Texas: Harcourt Brace & Company

Cone, James H. 1999. A black theology of liberation. Maryknoll, NY: Orbis Books.

Crawford, Janet Estridge. 1995. Rocking the Boat: Women's participation in the World Council of Churches 1948–1991. PhD Dissertation, Victoria University of Wellington.

Creswell, J. W. 2009. Research design: Qualitative, quantitative and mixed methods approaches. Los Angeles, CA: SAGE Publications.

Daloz, Laurent A. Parks, Cheryl H. Keen, James P. Keen and Sharon Daloz Parks. 1996. Common fire: Leading lives of commitment in a complex world. Boston, Mass: Beacon Press Books.

Dart, John. 2001. "Church Women (Dis)united." Christian Century, 118, no.1 (January 3, 2001). Religion and Philosophy Collection, EBSCOhost (accessed June 29, 2010).

Davis, Angela Y. 1983. Women, race and class. New York: Vintage Books.

Denzin, N. K. 1978. The research act: A theoretical introduction to sociological methods. 2nd ed. New York, NY: McGraw-Hill.

Denzin, N. K. and Y. S. Lincoln, 2008. Strategies of qualitative inquiry. Thousand Oaks, CA: Sage Publications.

Dinkelspiel, Anne. 1981. "On our way together: An update on the relationship between the Center for Women and Church Women United." Journal of Women and Religion, 1 no.1 (March 1, 1981): 36–37. ATLA Religion Database with ATLA Serials, OO host. (accessed June 29, 2010).

Doohan, Leonard. 2007. Spiritual leadership: The quest for integrity. New York/Mahwah, NJ.: Paulist Press.

Dorrien, Gary. 2007. "Rauschenbusch's Christianity and the Social Crisis." The Christian Century,29. Christian Century Foundation. Online preparation by Ted and Winnie Brock. http://www.religion-online.org/showarticle.asp?title=3501.

Ellacuria, Ignacio, S.J., and Jon Sobrino, S. J. eds. 1993. Mysterium liberationis: Fundamental concepts of liberation theology. Maryknoll, NY: Orbis Books.

Erdozain, Placido. 1981. Archbishop Romero, martyr of Salvador. Maryknoll, NY: Orbis Books.

Findlay, James F. 1993. Church people in the struggle: National Council of Churches and the black freedom movement. 1950–1970. New York: Oxford University Press.

Firebaugh, Glen. 2008. Seven rules for social research. Princeton, New Jersey: Princeton University Press.

Fitts, Leroy. 1985. The history of black Baptists. Nashville, Tennessee: Broadman Press.

FitzGerald, Thomas E. 2004. The ecumenical movement: An introductory history. Westport, Ct: Praeger Publishers.

Forbes, James. 2010. Interview with author. Seattle, WA. February 2011.

Friere, Paulo. 1973. Education for critical consciousness. New York: Seabury.

Gaines, Kevin K. 2006. Uplifting the race: Black leadership, politics, and culture in the twentieth century. Chapel Hill: The University of North Carolina Press.

Garrow, David J. 1986. Bearing the cross: Martin Luther King, Jr., and the Southern Christian Leadership Conference. New York: William Morrow.

Glaser, B. G. 1992. Basics of grounded theory analysis: Emergence vs. forcing. Mill Valley, CA: Sociology Press.

Grimm, Roberta J. and Kathleen S. Hurty. 2004. Prayer, power, and prophetic action: Church Women United in tapestry of justice, service, and unity. Arleon Kelly ed. 2004, 71–102. Tacoma, WA: National Association of Ecumenical and Interreligious Staff Pr, 2004. ATLA Religion Database with ATLA Serials, EBSCO host (accessed June 29, 2010).

Hartman, Marty, and Liz McDaniel. 2011. Interviewed by Phyllis I. Beaumonte. Seattle, WA. August. 2011.

Hamel, J., S. Dufour, and D. Fortin. 1993. Case study methods. Newbury Park, CA: SAGE.

Heifetz, Ronald A., and Marty Linsky. 2002. Leadership on the line. Boston, Mass: Harvard Business School Press.

Hennelly, Alfred T., S.J. 1997. Liberation theologies: The global pursuit of justice. Mystic, Conn: Twenty-Third Publications.

Hessel, Dieter T. 1972. A social action primer. Philadelphia: The Westminster Press.

Hopkins, Dwight N., and Linda E. Thomas, eds. 2009. Walk together children: Black and womanist theologies, church and theological education. Eugene, Oregon: Wipf & Stock Publishers.

Hull, Debra B. 2008. "Mossie Allman Wyker: Ordained to change the world." Discipliana, 67, No.12, 3–25 (March 1, 2008): ATLA Religion Database with ATLA Serials, EBSCO host (accessed June 29, 2010).

Introduction to Theology in an Ecumenical Context. 1993. The Lutheran federation and the Catholic church, 3–4. Seattle, WA: Seattle University.

Jones, Serene, and Paul Lakeland, eds. 2005. Constructive theology: A contemporary approach to classic themes. Minneapolis, MN: Augsburg Fortress.

Kelly, Arleon L., ed. 2004. A tapestry of justice, service, and unity: Local ecumenism in the United States, 1950–2000. Tacoma, WA: National Association of Ecumenical and Interreligious Staff Press.

Kenton, Jessie K., 2000. Church Women United in the Seattle area: Unpublished manuscript, Washington State Women's History Archive, Tacoma, WA.

Kenton, Jessie K., Lemuel Alva Peterson, William B. Cate, and Elaine J.W. Stanovsky. 1996. The story of the Church Council of Greater Seattle, 1919–1995: Generation to generation. Olympia, WA: Pan Press.

King, Coretta Scott. 1969. My life with Martin Luther King, Jr. New York: Henry Holt and Company.

King, Coretta Scott. 1993. The Martin Luther King, Jr. companion. New York: St. Martin's Press.

King, Martin Luther, Jr. 1986. Letter from a Birmingham Jail. In King: The making of a legend, ed. Gary Puckrein, 52–59. Washington, DC: The Vision Foundation.

King, Martin Luther, Jr., and the Southern Christian Leadership Conference. 1986. Bearing the cross. New York: Vintage Books.

Kinnamon, Michael. 1983. Towards visible unity: World Council of Churches and Commission on Faith and Order. Geneva: World Council of Churches.

Kinnamon, Michael. 1988. Truth and community: Diversity and its limits in the ecumenical movement. Grand Rapids, MI.: W. B. Eerdmans.

Kinnamon, Michael, and Thomas F. Best. 1985. Called to be one in Christ: United churches and the ecumenical movement Geneva, Switzerland: World Council of Churches.

Kinnamon, Michael and Brian E. Cope. 1997. The ecumenical movement: An anthology of key texts and voices. Geneva, Switzerland: World Council of Churches.

Krueger, Richard A., and Mary Anne Casey. 2000. Focus groups: A practical guide for applied research. 3rd ed. Thousand Oaks, CA: Sage Publications.

May, Melanie A. 1989. Bonds of unity: Women, theology, and the worldwide church. American Academy of Religion Academy Series. Atlanta, GA: Scholars Press.

Mays, Benjamin. 1950. A social gospel for the social awakening (Selections from the writings of Walter Rauschenbusch). New York: A Haddam House Book.

McGee, Henry W., Jr. 2007. "Seattle's central district, 1990–2006: Integration or displacement?" The Urban Lawyer. 39. No.2: 167–256.

McGee, Henry W., Jr. 2010. "Wealthy disparity pushes urban citizens of color to the nearby suburbs." The Seattle Times, December 28.

McKinney, William. 1994. Interview with Doris Anne (Dodie) Younger. In The responsibility people: Eighteen senior leaders of Protestant churches and national ecumenical agencies reflect on church leadership, 350–377. Grand Rapids, MI: W. B. Eerdmans.

Miles, M., and M. Huberman. 1978. Qualitative analysis: An expanded source book. Thousand Oaks, CA: SAGE Publications.

Miles, M., and M. Huberman. 1984. Qualitative data analysis: A source book for new methods. Thousand Oaks, CA: Sage Publications.

Moustakas, C. E. 1990. Heuristic research: Design, methodology, and application. Newbury Park, CA: SAGE Publications.

Niebuhr, Richard H. 1951. The kingdom of God in America. New York: Harper and Brothers.

Niebuhr, Richard H. 1951. Christ and culture. New York: Harper and Brothers.

Oberschall, Anthony. 1973. Social conflict and social movements. Englewood Cliffs, N.J.: Prentice-Hall.

O'Reilly, Bill. 2007. Culture warrior. New York: Doubleday Broadway Publishing Group.

Patton, M. Q. 1980. Qualitative evaluation methods. Beverly Hills, CA: SAGE.

Poor, Penny. 1983. "CWU to monitor emergency rooms." The Source, no. 5, (January, 4). Seattle, WA: Church Council of Greater Seattle.

Potter, Philip. 1981. Life in all its fullest. Geneva, Switzerland: World Council of Churches.

Potter, Philip, A. J. Vanderbent, and Pauline Webb. 1984. Faith and faithfulness: Essays on contemporary ecumenical themes: A tribute to Philip A. Potter. Geneva, Switzerland: World Council of Churches.

Ramos, Michael. 2011. Interview by author. Seattle, WA. September, 2010.

Rauschenbusch, Walter. 1914. Dare we be Christians. New York: Pilgrim Press.

Rauschenbusch, Walter.1917. A theology for the social gospel. New York: MacMillan.

Remy, Richard C. 1990. Government in the United States. Mission Hills, CA: Glencoe.

Salmon, J. 2010. On line interviews in real time. Los Angeles, CA: Sage Publications.

Schaefer, Mae. 1988. "Assignment: Poverty of women." The Source, vol.13, no.1. (February, 4). Seattle, WA. Church Council of Greater Seattle.

Shannon, Margaret, Carolyn L. Stang, and Billie Ann Wilson. 1977. Just because: The story of the national movement of Church Women United in the U.S.A., 1941–1975. Corte Madera, CA: Omega Books.

Sobrino, Jon. 1990. Archbishop Romero: Memories and reflections. Trans. Robert R. Barr. Maryknoll, NY: Orbis Books.

The Source. 1986. "World day of prayer." The Source, vol.10, no. 6, 4. (February). Seattle, WA: Church Council of Greater Seattle.

The Source. 1987. "Infant formula campaign continues: Infant health campaign." The Source vol.11, no.7, 4. (March). Seattle, WA: Church Council of Greater Seattle.

The Source. 1981. "Re-assignment race." The Source 10, no. 4 (February). Seattle, WA: Church Council of Greater Seattle.

Stakes, R. E. 1995. The art of case study research: Thousand Oaks, CA: Sage Publications.

Strauss, A. L. 1987. Qualitative analysis for social scientists. New York, NY: Cambridge University Press.

Strauss, A. L., and J. Corbin. 1990. Basis of qualitative research: Grounded theory procedures and techniques. Newbury Park, CA: SAGE Publications.

Swift, Mary. 2005. "Woman changing the world." King County Journal. January 9.

Taylor, Quintard. 1994. The forging of a black community: Seattle's central district from 1870 through the civil rights era. Seattle, WA: The University of Washington Press.

Thurman, Howard. 1976. Jesus and the disinherited. Boston, MA: Beacon Press.

Tull, James E. 1984. Martin Luther King Jr., civil Rights martyr. In Shapers of Baptist thought, 209–236. Macon, GA: Mercer University Press.

Tull, James E. 1984. "Walter Rauschenbusch, prophet of social Christianity." In Shapers of Baptist thought, 183–208. Macon, GA: Mercer University Press.

Van Manen, M. 1990. Researching lived experience: Human science for an action sensitive pedagogy. Albany, NY: SUNY Press.

Washington, James Melvin, ed. 1986. A testament of hope: The essential writing Martin Luther King, Jr. San Francisco, CA: Harper and Row.

Weber, Max. 1947. The theory of social and economic organization. London: Oxford University Press.

West, Cornell. 1997. Restoring hope: Conversations on the future of black America. Boston, MA: Beacon Press Books.

White, Ronald C. Jr., and C. Howard Hopkins. 1976. The social gospel: Religion and reform in changing America. Philadelphia, PA: Temple University Press.

Wiggins, Martha Lee. 2005. United Church Women: A constant drip of water will wear a hole in iron: The ecumenical struggle of church women to unite across race and shape the civil rights century. PhD diss., Union Theological Seminary.

Wyker, Mossie A. 1953. Church women in the scheme of things. Columbia, MO: Bethany Press.

Yin, R. 1984. Case study research: Design and methods. Newbury Park, CA: Sage.

Yin, R. 1989. Case study research: Design and methods. Rev. ed. Beverly Hills, CA: Sage Publications.

Yin, R. 1993. Applications of case study research. Beverly Hills, CA: Sage Publications.

Yin, R. 1994. Case study research: Design and methods. 2nd ed. Beverly Hills, CA: Sage Publications.

Zinn, Howard. 1995. A people's history of the United States: 1942–present. New York: Harper Perennial.

ABOUT THE AUTHOR

The author, Dr. Phyllis Ilene Ratcliff-Beaumonte, was born in Seattle, Washington. At the University of Washington she received a B.A. in Political Science and Editorial Journalism and an M.A. in Public Administration.

She answered her call to the Ministry and was licensed to preach in 1989. Later, in Berkeley, California, she was ordained at the National Baptist Women Ministers' regional convention. Dr. Arnelle Jackson, President, officiated. Dr. Beaumonte's theological preparation for ministry included an M.A. in Pastoral Studies and a Certificate in Pastoral Leadership from Seattle University's School of Theology and Ministry, and later a Doctor of Ministry from San Francisco Theological Seminary. She is currently serves as an Associate Minister at Seattle's Mount Zion Baptist Church.

Much of Dr. Beaumonte's mid-life was dedicated to teaching high school students, guest lecturing at Pacific Lutheran University, and serving as a part-time instructor at South Seattle Community College.

Weaving a Life of Faith with Social Justice: Church Women United in Seattle and Beyond encompasses her commitment to social justice and righteousness through her work with the Seattle and state units of Church Women United (CWU). Her love for CWU and its praxis is evident in the work she has done by writing this book to maintain its history and story.

Other publications

by the author include:

Satyagraha (1992), and

Roses and Thorns:

Poetry and Prose (1994).